Young, British and Muslim

Young, British and Muslim

PHILIP LEWIS

continuum

Continuum International Publishing Group

The Tower Building
11 York Road
London SE1 7NX
www.continuumbooks.com

80 Maiden Lane
Suite 704
New York NY 10038

First published 2007
Reprinted 2008

British Library Cataloguing-in-Publication Data
A catalogue record for this book is available from the British Library.

ISBN hb 0–8264–9729–2
9780826497291
pb 0–8264–9730–6
9780826497307

Library of Congress Cataloguing-in-Publication Data
Lewis, Philip.
Young, British, and Muslim/Philip Lewis
p. cm
Includes bibliographical references.
ISBN-13: 978-0-8264-9729-1
ISBN-13: 978-0-8264-9730-7 (pbk.)
ISBN-10: 0-8264-9729-2
ISBN-10: 0-8264-9730-6 (pbk.)
1. Muslims--Great Britain. 2. Muslims--Great Britain--Social conditions. 3. Intergenerational relations--Great Britain. 4. Great Britain--Ethnic relations. I. Title

Typeset by Fakenham Photosetting Limited, Fakenham, Norfolk
Printed and bound in Great Britain by Cromwell Press Ltd., Trowbridge, Wiltshire.

Contents

Acknowledgements

I am grateful to Rebecca Vaughan-Williams of Continuum for commissioning this work and her encouragement throughout, and to Nazily, Sadeq and Yahya for their generous and constructive comments. I have learned much from friends and colleagues involved in Bradford University's Programme for a Peaceful City, and honed many of my ideas in informal conversations with alumni of the Inter Cultural Leadership School. The Anglican Church to which I belong and for which I work as an Inter-faith Adviser has offered unfailing support and inspiration. My family – Faith, Tim and Naomi – with their characteristic insight and humour have enabled me to maintain a sense of perspective throughout.

Foreword

How is our society coping with the significant influx and development of Muslim populations in the United Kingdom? In turn, and as important, how are those populations managing to survive, prosper and integrate within British society? Sadly it seems to have taken the 9/11 attacks in the United States, and the London bombings of 7 July 2005 to spark the debate. But debate there now is, at last.

This book is a most welcome addition to the accumulating knowledge and understanding of issues that for far too long dared not speak their name. In the sixties and seventies we were somehow absolved or deflected from discussing Muslims in Britain by the often racially charged debate about immigration itself. Indeed the far right perceived the 'threat' to their sense of 'white Britain', more from the colour of the skin of those entering the country, than from their beliefs.

It may well be that the advent of mass economic immigration by exclusively white immigrants from Eastern Europe early in the twenty-first century has served to open a more intelligent period of discussion about both migration and integration. For many years we hid behind the concept that the majority of immigrants coming into Britain were simply Asian. Bradford was becoming an 'Asian city', whole electoral wards in Birmingham were Asian. But this was to oversimplify and indeed to obscure what was actually happening.

The Ugandan migration of Asians in the seventies, following their expulsion by Idi Amin, served to demonstrate over less than a generation how successful 'Asian' integration could be. The overwhelming majority of these 90,000 people were of Indian extraction and of British colonial experience. In retrospect they were tailor-made to succeed. The corner shop culture they generated – long hours, hard work, good service – soon developed; in the next generation, a group of highly educated, motivated individuals. The Ugandan Asians were no ordinary intake. They arrived, even if often dispossessed, a well educated entrepreneurial class.

Contrast them with the majority of Pakistani and Bangladeshi immigrants. They came from often very poor rural areas, under educated, and often from clusters of villages in which whole streets of people transposed themselves to cities like Blackburn and Bradford.

Research published in 2007 by IPPR suggests that Pakistani born immigrants are three times more likely to be on income support, and twice as likely to be on disability benefit than their British-born peers. Indian immigrants by contrast are less likely than British-born people to find themselves drawing either benefit.

It's not easy to side-step what else IPPR's figures show. The less successful waves of immigration tend to come from Muslim populations. Research in which I was involved at Channel 4 for a documentary called 'What Muslims Want', showed that young British Muslims tended to be more radical and more religious than their parents. Traits that have militated against further integration.

Add to this finding the phenomenal growth in television availability from South Asia and you discover something else. I have found in reporting on Muslim communities in Britain that indigenous South Asian languages are not only the lingua franca inside the family, but are the stuff of the daily television diet. It is very far from unusual to enter a Muslim family home to find the wide plasma screen in the corner is solely tuned to Urdu programming. For the children on the sofa, it is comfortable viewing – television focusing on people like themselves speaking a language they are more than familiar with.

Britain has allowed a series of separate and unequal societies to take root within its midst. These are communities in which this very separateness frequently limits the life chances, and reduces the opportunity for young people to share in the development of the wider society beyond. Only the shock of discovering that educated British-born Muslim men could find it in themselves to murder their compatriots by killing themselves in the name of Allah have we awoken to where the most extreme form of this disconnect can lead.

Young British and Muslim provides the context and many of the facts that must now be brought into play if we are to address what is a gathering crisis. It's not a crisis about Al Qaeda, nor indeed about suicide bombing. It's about us and the social cohesion within our society. Our signal failure to address what's happening has merely provided fodder for such extremism. For political parties that for so long have depended on leaders within these communities to deliver what in effect have often been 'block votes'; for well meaning do-gooders; for anti-racists, and beyond, the alert has been sounded. We ignore it at our own peril and at the peril of the communities involved.

Jon Snow
2007

Preface

Anyone picking up this book might ask why someone who is neither young nor Muslim should choose to write such a work at the present time. The first reason is that I have been working with Muslims for over twenty years in Bradford both as a practitioner of Christian–Muslim relations advising Anglican bishops, and an academic lecturing about Islam and the West, the last six years in the Peace Studies Department at Bradford University. Such sustained engagement with Muslim communities over many years means I can offer a perspective often missing in the avalanche of books, articles and media commentary which followed 9/11 and more specifically 7/7.

I mention Bradford, the epicentre of *The Satanic Verses* affair and the location of two serious riots in 1995 and 2001, because no one in such a city can pretend that relations between its growing young British, Muslim communities – many with ancestry in rural Kashmir – and non-Muslim communities are easy. I have written elsewhere of some of the many initiatives in the city which have sought to develop and deepen relations between young adults living, to some extent, parallel lives.[1]

My concern has been to write in a way that neither demonizes nor sentimentalizes Muslims. Ironically, my first book about Muslims in the early 1990s was an attempt to get a largely secular and left-liberal leaning 'race and ethnicity community' to take 'religion' seriously as a component of identity.[2] This book, contrariwise, worries that many politicians, journalists, policy-makers and academics have fallen into the opposite trap – namely, of privileging 'Islam' as an explanation for quite disparate phenomena, whether riots, disaffected inner-city youth, political radicalization or violent extremism.

Not only is Islam used to eclipse other identities, ethnic, class or professional, many of which Muslims share with their fellow-citizens, but Islam is in danger of being 'essentialized' (in the jargon of 'cultural studies') – reduced to some unchanging essence and pathologized. Indeed, a small but widely read group of political commentators talk of an 'Islamist threat' as 'the conflict of our times ... [whereby] the

West faces a challenge to its values, culture and freedoms as profound, in its way, as the threat posed by fascism and communism'.[3]

My objection is not to the need to expose certain Muslim traditions which both demonize and threaten the West – clearly, they do exist. My problem is rather that Islamism, also described as 'political Islam', is presented as an undifferentiated phenomenon. In reality, the category is complex. It can encompass, on the one hand, groups in Turkey who share political power and who are analogous to Christian Democrats in the European tradition, and, on the other, the likes of Al Qaeda, itself a hybrid phenomenon. In Britain, it includes a new generation of young activists who are, in some respects, post-Islamist, who are engaging pragmatically with public and civic life.

Another example will illustrate my anxieties. Recently, a programme was shown on the Channel 4 television series *Dispatches*, entitled 'Undercover Mosque' (15 January 2007). Its investigative journalist, over a period of four months, had filmed preachers, and identified DVDs and books circulating within the confines of a number of mosques, embodying bigoted, even incendiary anti-Western commentary, purporting to subvert democracy and preparing for jihad, while reviling Christians and Jews. Women were presented as congenitally deficient in intellect and deserving of physical punishment when transgressing Islamic dress codes. The main mosque chosen for exposure was in Birmingham and was influenced and funded by groups in Saudi Arabia. This version of Islam, which describes itself as Salafi – but is called Wahhabi by its critics – is austere, literalist and intolerant.

Saudi Arabia was an intellectual backwater of the Islamic world until the 1960s. Indeed, even today draconian punishments of lapidation, decapitation and amputation are still practised. The intellectual centres of the Islamic world, whether Cairo, Fez or Qom, had little time for such obscurantism. It is only massive subventions of oil wealth in the last thirty years which have projected this tradition world-wide.

Once again, I have no objection to exposing such pernicious and dangerous obscurantism. However, unless the viewer has a map of Islam on which she can locate this phenomenon, such exposure unwittingly contributes to generating fear of Muslims, who happen to be our neighbours. In reality, of more than a thousand mosques in Britain, only some forty belong to the main tradition highlighted in the programme – Ahl-i Hadith.[4] It is as if someone knowing nothing of Christianity in its diversity and complexity generalizes from

American Christian Zionist pamphlets vehemently opposing peace in Israel/Palestine and seeking to hasten Armageddon. Or, again, it is as if someone who knows nothing of Judaism generalizes from a trawl through Orthodox Jewish websites in Israel and the USA in the early 1990s, with their discussions about arcane Jewish legal categories such as *din rodef* – the duty to kill a Jew who imperils the life or property of another Jew.

Now, in reality, both Christian Zionism and extreme Orthodox Judaism are worthy of study and, of course, both are worrying. In the case of the former, significant political figures in the Bush administration seem to be sympathetic to it. Further, the arcane discussions of Jewish law were part of a concerted campaign to delegitimize Rabin's government and support those opposed to the Oslo Peace Process. Rabin's murderer, Yigal Amir, certainly took such religious guidelines seriously. Israeli society woke up after Rabin's assassination in 1995 to discover the existence of a self-contained theocratic subculture within its midst. Yet, at most 10 per cent of American Christians accept the Christian Zionist analysis and, at most, one in six Israeli Jews were either willing to condone Rabin's murder or refused to condemn it.

The second reason for writing this book is to enable non-Muslims to overhear some of the anguished and passionate intra-Muslim debates now exercising their communities, not least about their place in British society and the nature of leadership in the communities, religious, communal and political. It is clear to me that a significant inter-generational shift in leadership is occurring. This should not be a cause for surprise when we realize that of the 50 per cent of the community who are under 25 years old – the focus of this study – most were born and educated in the UK. This is in contrast to some 85 per cent of the Muslim elite, active as MPs, councillors and leaders of Muslim associations, who were born outside Britain.[5]

It is evident that British Muslims are beginning to contribute significantly to academic and policy debate. This is to be welcomed. Their contributions will surprise many by their candour. I have in front of me a fine book of essays, by a group of young Muslim academics, social scientists and Islamic specialists. Its title indicates its desire to address hard issues: *The State We Are In: Identity, Terror and the Law of Jihad*. The introduction, while offering a nuanced analysis of the responsibilities of government and media, points, within the Muslim communities, to

> *a genuine failure of leadership ... Local community 'elders' are propped up through artificial support mechanisms that facilitate the electoral process to the advantage of the main political parties but take out of the hands of the people the choice of who they want as their leaders. Religious leadership has also been weak. The imams in mainstream mosques are not central, if relevant at all, to the leadership of Muslims, never mind being responsible for radicalising of the young.*[6]

In seeking to make sense of the struggles of young British Muslims and to depict the communities in which many are embedded, I shall draw on a variety of perspectives offered by young Muslim academics, journalists, film-makers, activists, religious scholars and novelists. In addition, there is a burgeoning specialist literature with seminal contributions from historians, geographers, religious studies specialists and anthropologists. Throughout this study I have sought, where possible, to enable Muslims to speak for themselves. While I am aware of the structural constraints within which any minority, religious or ethnic, has to operate – the stuff of much social science commentary – I have tried to communicate something of the energy and creativity also evident within the Muslim communities, and often missing from such accounts.

My third reason for writing is to combat the notion that 'Islam' is at the root of every single problem within Muslim communities in Britain. Many of these problems have little to do with Islam and more to do with the dislocation wrought by migration or learning to live as a religious minority in an environment perceived as either indifferent or hostile. This sharpens the usual inter-generational tensions within any community.

The best study of the dislocation wrought by migration and its accompanying discontents is a wonderful work poignantly entitled *Lost In Translation*, by Eva Hoffman. Hoffman's families were secular Jews who, because of the persistence of anti-Semitism, left Poland in the 1950s for Canada. She describes her parents caught between nostalgia and alienation – nostalgia for the old country, which, of course, is no longer quite the same, and alienation from the new. She reflects that the only way migrants can escape marginalization is linguistic competence, enabling them to translate anger into argument. As she reflects on intra-community gang fights between Black and Hispanic groups, she also recognizes that some sections of migrant communities do not acquire such competence.

She is also alert to the loss of parental control of children. The latter are often the first generation to enjoy formal education but in a culture and language not shared with parents. Sons and daughters of migrants are often streetwise and better equipped than their parents to negotiate across cultures. There is also a plethora of novel ways of being 'religious' in the new context, where youth rub shoulders and study with co-religionists from many other parts of the world. As part of growing up and identity formation, they begin to experiment with a variety of new lifestyles on offer – religious and secular – and develop hybrid identities expressed in music and language quite alien to the experience of their parents. All of these phenomena we will see re-enacted in different ways by young British Muslims.

With regard to learning to live as a religious minority, non-Muslims forget that most Muslims have come from majority Muslim societies. Also, a majority have come from rural contexts where Islam was part of the rhythm of life, its prayer times and local festivals devoted to 'the friends of God' – dynasties of holy men accessible through shrines dotting the countryside – enriching its religious calendar. Islam, in short, was a largely unself-conscious part of a shared oral tradition. At its best, this tradition, often labelled Sufism, is a carrier of Islamic humanism. It is through the activities of such 'friends of God' and their devotees that Islam's vernacular devotional tradition was generated and Islam took root in the hearts and minds of ordinary believers, who lived outside the Arab-speaking heartlands and were unable to understand or access directly its Arabic sacred texts.

However, many parents and religious leaders, imported into Britain's mosques from the same rural socio-cultural world, are often at a loss to help their children answer questions about Islam posed by school friends, teachers or youth workers. A new generation of Muslims are searching for expressions of Islam which can connect with their lived experience as British Muslims whose first language is English. In short, Islam has had to become self-conscious and articulate in a new and bewildering culture which owes little or nothing to it.

If this is not difficult enough, the largest group of British Muslims, with roots in Pakistan, are sometimes referred to as the new Irish. This is because, as with the Irish, who migrated to England in the nineteenth and twentieth centuries, it is their history and ethnicity which separates them from the English, as well as their religion. The Irish did not quickly forget the many atrocities visited on Ireland by its English and Scottish colonizers – history which left a legacy of anti-Irish bigotry and racism in mainland Britain.

In a later chapter, it will become clear that there are parallels between religious formation in a Catholic seminary in 1950s England – a world whose passing few now regret but which is beautifully and movingly re-created in John Cornwell's recent autobiography[7] and their Islamic equivalents today. Cornwell's world was characterized by a defiant conservatism, hostile to an England contemptuously dismissed as heretical and pagan; a world where Guy Fawkes could be re-invented as part of a glorious story of fortitude which one day would find its reward as England rediscovered its true faith. Such fantasies of the apologetic imagination are also entertained by some Muslim groups.

Now, of course, Catholicism in Britain has always been more expansive than its Irish embodiment. Today, the Catholic tradition also anticipates many of the challenges confronting Islam. Again, it is Cornwell who has identified them with his usual candour. The need to address the continued disdain for women and their role within the faith; changing attitudes of the younger generations towards authority as many have moved out of Catholic enclaves; how to live in pluralist communities that actively respect differing beliefs and value systems; competing images of the Church in uneasy co-existence, such as the new metaphor of the Church as pilgrim people on the move or the old metaphor of the 'triumphalist citadel'. There is a defensive climate within conservative groups, which prefer to portray the Church as the victim of media persecution, rather than engage self-criticism to avoid collusion with 'denial and dysfunction'.[8] As we reflect on the different visions of what it means to be a Muslim in Britain today that are competing for a hearing from young Muslims, we will notice many of these same issues, albeit in Islamic dress.

By the end of this book, we will have reason to remember the sub-title of Eva Hoffman's meditation on migration: *Life in a New Language*. I think of one of my brightest students, a young Muslim woman whose rural Kashmiri parents had little or no formal education. In one generation, the community, availing themselves of the educational opportunities afforded in Britain, are generating a new leadership. Here was someone who had developed the skills and confidence to be one of the leaders of the anti-war movement in the city, addressing huge mixed crowds. Amidst a cacophony of Muslim voices, I hope to render such constructive interventions audible. Such voices are fashioning new expressions of Muslim identity, at ease in

British society. Such quiet engagement is a vital antidote to the high-profile media cases of extremist jihadi cells of young men accused of various horrendous crimes, whether intending to blow up aeroplanes or to brutalize British Muslim soldiers.

Notes

1. P. Lewis, 'Faith in the City. Religious and Secular Traditions Collaborating to Limit the Appeal and Impact of Radical Islam: Bradford, a Case-Study', forthcoming in *Aberystwyth Journal of World Affairs*.

2. P. Lewis, *Islamic Britain: Religion, Politics and Identity among British Muslims*, 2nd edn (London: I. B. Tauris, 2002).

3. M. Gove, *Celsius 7/7* (London: Weidenfeld and Nicolson, 2006), pp. 2–3.

4. In a 1998 survey of 321 mosques in Britain, only 18 belonged to this tradition. See C. Peach, 'Muslims in the 2001 Census of England and Wales: Gender and Economic Disadvantage', *Ethnic and Racial Studies*, 29 (2006), p. 641.

5. J. Klausen, *The Islamic Challenge: Politics and Religion in Western Europe* (Oxford: Oxford University Press, 2005), p. 23.

6. T. Abbas, 'Introduction', in Aftab Ahmad Malik (ed.), *The State We Are In: Identity, Terror and the Law of Jihad* (Bristol: Amal Press, 2005), pp. xiii–xiv.

7. See J. Cornwell, *Seminary Boy* (London: Fourth Estate, 2006).

8. J. Cornwell, *Breaking Faith: Can the Catholic Church Save Itself?* (New York: Penguin Compass, 2001), pp. 7–9.

Introduction

In the course of an engaging memoir – *Only Half of Me: Being a Muslim in Britain* – the broadcaster Rageh Omaar struggles to make sense of what drove the British-born bombers of 7/7 or the would-be bombers of 21/7. The latter were all child immigrants who had arrived in England within the previous ten years, fleeing wars in the Horn of Africa – just as Omaar's family had fled Somalia in 1972.

What is evident is that Omaar, at many points, is no clearer than many non-Muslims as to why this happened. Understandably, he also worries that Islam and British Muslims will be defined and represented to British society though the lens of such atrocities. Further, since a 'war on terror' presupposes a defined enemy, British Muslims are asking: 'Do you know who among *us* are your allies? Are all of us suspect? If not, then who is on *our* side?'[1]

This question, articulated by a popular, Oxbridge-educated, London-based, ex-BBC journalist, now with Al-Jazeera, is echoed by a working-class British Muslim of Pakistani ancestry in Bradford. In a series of conversations with a group of young British Pakistani men compiled by a British novelist – *Made in Bradford* – one of them remarks:

> *9/11 has really put pressure on us, not because we're Pakistani, but as Muslims. Government's always questioning everything we do, these days. What goes on in mosques, in homes, in schools – everywhere. It's like us, as Muslims, we're Public Enemy Number One. It gets to you. It's bound to get to you. You try to shrug it off but it keeps coming back at you, keeps getting worse.*[2]

The complexity and dynamism of Britain's Muslim communities, with their multiplicity of identities, stories, ethnicities and migration histories, is in danger of being reduced to one 'singular affiliation'. Amartya Sen, a Nobel Prize winner in economics, has recently warned against the potential lethal impact of such 'miniaturisation of people'. Sen's passion to resist the obliteration of 'the intricacies of plural groups and multiple loyalties' is grounded in a formative experience as an eleven-year-old in Bengal, where he saw a poor Muslim day-labourer murdered by Hindu fanatics during inter-communal riots for no reason other than his religious affiliation.[3]

Omaar sees the same process of miniaturization at work in the mind of Mohammed Siddique Khan, the thirty-year-old leader of the 7/7 group. Why did he choose to detonate his bomb at Edgware Road tube station, the heart of the largest Arab Muslim district of London? Omaar speculates that he did so because Edgware Road

> *represented a relationship between Islam and the West, a cultural and ideological abomination to those who believe in the pure interpretation of Al Qaeda's message. They were attacking the idea that Islam as a religion and Muslims as a community can thrive in the West ... They were attacking the idea that you can have a British identity but still be part of the wider global 'nation of believers'. The belief that a western city can ever be a part of the modern story of Islam ... is sacrilegious to the fundamentalist vision.*[4]

We will discover that there are many more British Muslims from a variety of ethnic backgrounds beginning to articulate an alternative set of Islamic narratives – traditionalist, progressive, Islamist, Sufi – which resist this false polarity. However, we will also encounter tendencies and groups within the Muslim communities which, wittingly or unwittingly, collude in such a Manichaean world-view.

A need for religious literacy

Islam as a religion and civilization has embedded itself in six distinct linguistic and geographical zones: Arab, Black African, Persian, Turkic, South Asian and Malay – indeed, there are more Indonesian Muslims than Arab Muslims.[5] Most of these worlds have contributed to the kaleidoscope of communities in Britain. Needless to say, these communities carry with them quite distinct histories and attitudes to Britain and the West. Many Arabs in London are better thought of as international commuters – with parts of London dubbed 'Beirut-on-Thames' by journalists, the playground of the wealthy who have bought property there. This contrasts with other communities, often 'poor, alienated and intertwined [by family ties] with the hungriest and angriest parts of the Muslim world'.[6]

There are probably 125,000 Turks in Britain, most in North-East London, from the mainland and Cyprus.[7] Turkey was never colonized; rather, it was itself a great imperial power for half a millennium, encompassing much of the Middle East and swathes of South-East Europe. Turks do not define themselves over against Europe and the West; indeed, they are part of NATO. Further, for more than eighty years they have been influenced by a French 'secularism' which seeks to empty public and civic life of religious symbols and formal influence. A recent study of 250 young Kurds and Turks in London found that being Muslim was subsumed within cultural identity and 'sixty-eight per cent did not subscribe to any religious identity at all'.[8]

In contrast, Muslim communities with roots in South Asia were colonized, and often define themselves over against, their erstwhile Western colonizers. One Islamic tradition, named after its place of origin, Deoband, a country town some ninety miles north-east of Delhi, which has created some 18 institutions in England to train religious leaders – *'ulama* – emerged soon after the 'mutiny' in India.[9] Some of its founders, involved in this unsuccessful 'jihad', conceived of Deoband as, in part, equipping religious leaders for a new jihad if and when the time proves propitious.[10] Deoband has generated pietist and activist streams, with the Taliban a recent product of this latter tradition. In a later chapter, we will map the emergence of two conflicting narratives within this school of thought in Britain. One remains deeply suspicious of wider society, the other urges a principled engagement.

No one is a Muslim-in-general

Ideally, 'Muslim' should remain in inverted commas throughout this book to leave open what exactly is meant by such a term. For some, their 'Muslimness' is as much 'cultural' as religious, if these two terms can be prised apart for purposes of analysis. For others, it is a vehicle of 'identity politics', the dynamics of which will be explored in a later chapter. For those who privilege religious commitment over ethnicity, parental culture, or 'identity politics' this can have diverse expressions – mystic, missionary, militant or some combination of these.[11]

We need to remember that the generality of male Muslims confine their religious devotions to Friday prayer and occasional daily prayer as and when they can. Women are still largely excluded from the majority of mosques. Probably no more than 5 per cent of British Muslims belong to self-consciously Muslim organizations apart from the mosque. However, the culture of the first generation of migrants necessarily reflects Islamic influence. Many South Asian taxi-drivers frequently play the popular *qawwali*s by the late Nusrat Fateh Ali Khan. The *qawwali* belongs to a genre of spiritual songs in praise of God, his Prophet and the 'friends of God', with roots deep in Indian Islamic history, at least as far back as the twelfth century. These vernacular hymns emerged from within the world of Sufism and its shrines. Drawing on the imagery of rural society and its folk ballads, they became vehicles of popular devotion. They explain, in part, how a religious tradition whose scriptures are in Arabic were mediated to and rooted in the hearts and minds of the majority of Muslims who were not Arab-speaking.

Dynasties of holy men, organized into local, regional and transnational orders, also generated a religiosity of localized solidarity, healing and intercession centred around shrines which over centuries drew non-Muslims into their orbit. Studies have shown how, for example, non-Muslim tribes in India were in the course of a few hundred years 'Islamized' – evident in the shift to Muslim names – with the shrine and Sufi cult as the main instrument of acculturation.[12] Needless to say, this gives the lie to the taunt that Islam invariably spread by the sword.[13] The Muslim holy man, usually referred to as *Shaykh* or *Pir* – the Arabic and Persian for 'elder' – remains an influential figure in local communities. In a recent, entertaining novel set in Manchester exploring the world and rivalries of Pakistani restaurateurs, the central character, the worldly-wise 'curry king of Manchester', is depicted at times of crisis as visiting his *Pir* -a figure sympathetically drawn by the novelist.[14]

Nusrat Fateh Ali Khan frequently visited the UK giving concerts to adoring crowds, some of whom would spontaneously break into ecstatic dance. He developed the art form of *qawwali* and combined it with modern film music. Such music has partly been reinvented for a new generation of British Muslims by young artists such as Sami Yusuf, a young Mancunian in his twenties of Azheri ethnicity, who sings in English and who plays to sell-out crowds. Writing of Nusrat Fateh Ali Khan ten years ago, a young journalist noted that 'through the use of his music, [he] effectively combats the puritan voices which have wished to eliminate all aesthetic and recreational elements from Muslim life'.[15] This could be said of Sami Yusuf also.

Yusuf Islam – formerly the singer Cat Stevens – was drawn into a puritan form of Islam which eschewed music, considered un-Islamic. As a result, 'he famously destroyed his instruments and stopped making new records for nearly two decades following advice from

Muslim religious scholars [including Suhaib Hasan] that doing so would be sinful'.[16] Suhaib Hasan, a leader of the South Asian Ahl-i Hadith movement, close to the Saudi Wahhabi tendency, featured in the *Dispatches* programme 'Undercover Mosque'. The Deobandis, a mainstream, South Asian Sunni tradition which has been most successful in creating large numbers of institutions in England for religious formation and the creation of *'ulama*, shares the Ahl-i Hadith and Wahhabi view that music is prohibited. Given the importance of music for young people, this prohibition renders its task of connecting with British Muslims that much more difficult.

All too often, journalistic and political commentary on Islam supposes that actual ethnic particularities are subordinate to the aspirational rhetoric of belonging to one, undivided, world-wide community – the *umma*. The reality is quite different. In landmark studies of Muslim communities in London and nationally, a social geographer rehearses recent Labour Force Survey data for 1997–2002 which 'showed 98 per cent of Bangladeshi women, 94 per cent of Pakistani women and 92 per cent of Indian women were married to co-ethnics'. Further, he found that within the capital 'there are fracture lines between the largest Muslim ethnic groups. Bangladeshi Muslims, who form London's largest Muslim group, are highly encapsulated, showing little residential mixing with other [Muslim] groups. White Muslims and Black Caribbean Muslims are separated from both Indian and Pakistani Muslims. The *Ummah* ... is not manifested in residential terms.'[17]

While common religious affiliation can be a far more effective vehicle for large-scale mobilization than nationality, such solidarities tend to be short-lived and related to specific issues, whether *The Satanic Verses* affair in 1989 or the Danish cartoons in 2006. Muslim everyday life, by contrast, is rooted in narrower loyalties of caste, clan and sect: 'The Pakistani or the Bangladeshi or the Indian or the African Muslims' *weltanschauung* [critical] of the West's treatment of the Middle East is shared, but not their daughters.'[18]

Specific social and intellectual challenges facing 'Muslims' as a minority

With the exception of Muslims from India and East Africa, most Muslims have migrated from societies where Islam is taken for granted as a component of society, culture, legal and political institutions. In Britain – as in the West generally – Muslims are having to discover how to be a Muslim as a minority in a non-Muslim society, either indifferent to Islam or, since 9/11 and 7/7, increasingly suspicious about Muslim intentions.

It is worth recalling that Islamic jurisprudence (*fiqh*) did not envisage minority Muslim communities formed by voluntary economic migration from Muslim lands to non-Muslim countries. Over a quarter of a century ago, the late Dr Zaki Badawi lamented the fact that Sunni 'Muslim theology offers, up to the present, no systematic formulation of the status of being in a minority'.[19] A distinguished Indian scholar also observed that with the exception of the recent trauma of colonialism, 'Sunni Muslims took power and dominance for granted. They knew either how to command or to obey. They had, through most of their history, rarely learned *to live with others in equality and fraternity*'.[20] He was so concerned with the lack of such critical thinking in a world where possibly one in three Muslims now live as minorities that he created the *Journal for Muslim Minority Affairs*.

Living in a society in which Muslims are a minority requires investment in institutions and an understanding of the need for fresh thinking. A distinguished South African scholar has identified the enormity of the challenge this poses:

> *The body of thought that the project of rethinking ... attempts to confront is premised on a triumphalist ideology: an age when Islam was a political entity and an empire. A cursory glance at this intellectual legacy will show how this ideology of Empire permeates theology, jurisprudence, ethics, and espouses a worldview that advances hierarchy. What adds to the frustration of millions of followers of Islam is the fact that this triumphalist creed and worldview is unable to deliver its adherents to its perceived goals of worldly success and leadership.*[21]

In conversation, this scholar told me he was working on a book with the poignant title *After Empire*. The challenge was to disengage the religious disciplines from the imperial narrative in which they were embedded, since that narrative was now dysfunctional. He too, like his mentor, the late Professor Fazlur Rahman of the University of Chicago, anticipated opposition from 'proponents of radical Islam [for whom] the intellectual pursuit of Islam, especially in non-traditional institutions such as universities and colleges, is a new form of Orientalism ... [Such] paranoia is pervasive.'[22]

Nor are Muslims well equipped for interfaith dialogue with Christians. One of the few British Muslim scholars who has actually studied Christianity observed that 'a frank supersessionism written into the Islamic tradition leaves little need for "curiosity" about "the otherness of the other"'.[23] In a Catholic journal he noted that:

> *In the Islamic tradition an* alim *[religious scholar] or a* mufti *[legal specialist] is required to have some basic knowledge and . . . an awareness of the custom (*'urf*) and 'practice' (*adat*) of the people where he lives and work[s] . . . [Yet] in Europe, I am not aware of any madrasa which is in the business of training* 'ulama *[in] even the basic concepts and ideas of the Judaeo-Christian traditions . . . Furthermore, there is an urgent need to introduce the intellectual and cultural trends of Western society into Muslim seminaries' syllabi.*[24]

Nevertheless, there remains a paucity of academic centres in either the Muslim world or in Islamic institutions in Britain which study Western intellectual, cultural and religious traditions. Many commentators have pointed out that very few Muslim students study the humanities – history, literature, modern languages (with the exception of Arabic), political and social sciences – opting instead for vocational courses such as law, engineering, accountancy, dentistry, medicine and business. A friend in Manchester, who was the first youth worker from a Bangladeshi background in the North-West, recently told me that there were still only a handful fifteen years on. This means there are relatively few Muslims in community development, youth work, teaching, social work and counselling who can help young Muslims negotiate the many challenges of living in British society, whether across cultures or across generations.

Inter-generational tensions

Clan and patriarchy

A young sociologist reflecting on deprivation among South Asian Muslims in Britain sees it as

> *compounded by the traditional rural origins of first-generation migrants, who have largely organised community and political culture around clan-based kinship networks [*biradari*, 'brotherhood'], where opportunities for the subsequent generations to break out do not always exist. Local Muslim leadership is weak, and inter-generational*

> *tensions are not being resolved, particularly in relation to patriarchy . . . [Many young Muslims] are trapped in a cycle of decline and are far removed from the growing body of high-income, well-integrated and savvy class of professional Muslims.*[25]

Clans as an organizing social system are integral to many societies from which Muslims in Britain have migrated. A comparative study of Somalis in London and Toronto makes clear the extent to which clans remain an organizing principle in diaspora communities. However, even London was not as divided as Toronto, where there were 'no fewer than thirty Somali community organizations, each dedicated to assisting the absorption and resettlement of Somali refugees, most declaring that their services are intended for all Somalis, and almost all knowing that in fact only those of a particular group or sub-clan will actually approach them'.[26]

Anger at the continuing impact of clan and patriarchal attitudes in the West, often underwritten by much traditional Muslim scholarship, informs the work of a growing number of female writers, such as the Dutch-Somali writer Ayaan Hirsi Ali, or the Canadian South Asian Irshad Manji, or the Black American academic Amina Wadud. Ali has given up on Islam as a result, Manji is hanging on by her fingernails, while Wadud is arguing from within the tradition for root-and-branch reform.[27]

Once again, we see an inter-generational struggle across the Muslim communities, where young British Muslims are challenging, in the name of 'professionalism', the dominance of *biradari*/clan politics in community centres, local politics and mosques. The battle is far from won: some weary of the struggle and become disillusioned, but many persevere. Occasionally, these struggles hit the national media, as with the attempt in Birmingham by some South Asian *biradaris* to subvert the electoral process by manipulating postal votes[28] – a ploy exposed by, *inter alia*, a young female Muslim lawyer. More recently, Channel 4, in a *Dispatches* programme titled 'Women-Only Jihad', covered attempts by young activists to force mosques to open their doors to women.[29]

From a rural to an urban religiosity

A majority of Muslims who migrated to the UK in the 1950s and 1960s were from rural societies. What is frequently overlooked is that the shift from rural to urban – within or outside the Muslim world – entails major shifts in religiosity. A seminal study of this was undertaken by a German anthropologist who studied observable changes in religiosity between Muslims in an Anatolian village – 'Subay' (not its real name) – and their relatives who had migrated to a German city.

We can consider his broad conclusions as they affect what religious studies specialists identify as the four 'domains' of any religion – discourse, practice, community and institution. In 'Subay' the key religious functionary who embodies the religious institution, and interprets Islamic 'discourse', conducts worship, and enacts normative 'practice', is the imam of the mosque. In the village, society and Islamic 'community' are coterminous:

> *During secular times, the village appears to be comprised of a group of largely autonomous households which base their relationships on the values of honour . . . and observe the reciprocal exchange of offerings and provocations. During sacred times (the five times of prayer, Friday mornings, the month of fasting . . . the great religious feasts), this society changes into a religious community. Through Islamic rituals, a social structure is established in which one does not stand in opposition to one's fellow man but rather beside him; in which one does not preserve one's honour against the others but collectively honours God; in which one does not exchange but shares; in which goods are given not because of mutual obligation but because of need; in which not competition and conflict but unity reigns.*[30]

The secular and sacred order are deemed complementary. The peasants realize that both elements are important. Without 'fear of God' might is right even in a village. Without political-legal constraints, 'fear of God' is not enough. To have status in the village the notable must have standing in both systems: 'One must be a Muslim as well as the member of a family whose honour and reputation is indisputable'.[31]

Religious practice is deemed the responsibility of the heads of family, who fast during Ramadan, while the young men are excused this obligation when it falls in midsummer, since they have to thresh the fields. Derelictions of religious duties, such as missed prayers and fasting, are seen as debts which can be discharged later in life. Many elderly men rise early to make up prayers neglected during their youth. Most believe that the reintroduction of Islamic law in Turkey would be desirable but do not see it as effecting some radical social transformation. Interestingly, they do not dispute the conclusions of a republican-minded migrant who claims this would set the country back fifty years!

Within the village, participation in ritual practice is not simply an expression of an individual's relationship to God but also a claim to belong to the community. One young man feels that much of their religiosity lacks the 'right intention', a precondition for its legitimacy. The imam might forbid something but they ignore him because everyone else ignores him too!

The shift to a German town sees major changes in all four domains. Religious community and society are now no longer complementary realities. The former now becomes a religious enclave in an indifferent or hostile society. Those whose religiosity was lukewarm in 'Subay' can and do drift away from any participation in Germany. There are many more ways of being Muslim on offer in Germany, ranging from militant Islamist groups, banned in Turkey, to Sufi groups, as well as an apolitical devotional movement with roots in India. Religiosity is less likely to be external and formal, but often becomes more self-conscious and dependent on choice.

Further, the imam has lost his monopoly as the man who is taken for granted as institutional leader. The institutional domain is now crowded and contested. So the religious community becomes fragmented around different responses to this new social situation. The role of the mosque also changes. In addition to being a place for worship, it is the place where the Turkish language and culture is also passed on to a new generation of children educated and socialized in German schools. Islamic symbols also assume different meanings. This is especially clear with regard to Islamic law. In 'Subay' it was seen as an inevitable part of what it means to be a Muslim. In Germany, the reintroduction of Islamic law is freighted with millenarian hopes, where its absence is presented as an all-embracing explanation for evil, whether in Turkey or Germany. We are well on the way to seeing the distinction being drawn between a secular nation-state and a 'religious utopia' – a distinction which is incomprehensible to the mainstream Islamic legal and intellectual tradition, although such zealotry has always existed on the margins.

In Britain, a significant number of Muslim migrants are from educated, urban backgrounds, like Rageh Omaar's family. However, the majority come from rural contexts which approximate in many particulars to 'Subay'. Their children and grandchildren, who are British-educated and socialized in a vastly different social, intellectual and cultural world, are busily experimenting with a diversity of lifestyles, including expressions of Islam quite different from those of their parents. Since a large majority of mosques continue to be the preserve of the elders, the majority of religious practitioners in the mosques – the *'ulama* – are still imported from their parents' home country. Such *'ulama*, whether or not they are well educated in the traditional Islamic sciences, generally have minimal understanding of British society and the issues facing young British Muslims.

The more religiously serious turn to other groups or the Internet to look for answers to what it means to be Muslim. This becomes a lottery. If they are lucky, they will be drawn into movements which are keen to help them engage responsibly with wider society; if they are unlucky, they will be drawn into the orbit of groups which preach disengagement or defiance of wider society. Others silently distance themselves from active involvement in a religious world deemed irrelevant.

Islamic practices in Britain: set menu or à la carte?

Surveys and polls of Muslim opinion in Britain routinely suggest that young British Muslims in the 16–24 age group are religiously more conservative than their parents and grandparents. There is widespread opposition to British foreign policy, a greater ambivalence towards the perpetrators of 7/7 and increased susceptibility to conspiracy theories. One survey suggests that half of 18- to 24-year-olds believe America and Israel were responsible for 9/11, while 41 per cent have convinced themselves that Princess Diana was killed to stop her marrying a Muslim.[32]

A consistently higher percentage of 16- to 24-year-olds, compared to their elders, favour Islamic state schools over secular schooling, would prefer women to wear head covering and deem Islamic law preferable to British law. What shocked commentators was the discovery that over a third of young Muslims agree with a particular formulation of *sharia*, to the effect that 'Muslim conversion is forbidden and punishable by death'.[33]

We will return in a later chapter to provide a context for such data and to attempt to make sense of the sources of anger and alienation which many young Muslims articulate. However, a number of preliminary comments can be made. The same surveys suggest that, despite fears of rising Islamophobia, 84 per cent of all Muslims feel that they have been treated fairly in British society. We will need to explore the reasons for this mismatch of fear and reality.

Two recent surveys suggest that between 78 and 86 per cent of Muslims affirm that Islam is important to them. However, these same two surveys include contradictory data as to whether such attitudes translate into regular worship. The first reports that 48 per cent never attend mosque and 6 per cent only do so on special occasions, while 19 per cent pray once a week. The remaining quarter are more regular, praying between two to seven times a week. This is hard to square with the figures advanced in the later survey, which indicate that 49 per cent pray five times a day![34]

When young British Muslims assert a preference for Islamic law over British law, we need to remember the observation that, for Muslims in diasporas, *sharia* can be seen as a utopian project. Had the question been posed as follows: 'What do you know about *sharia* and what aspects of it do you especially value?', it is unlikely that many would have mentioned the issue of 'apostasy laws'. In much of the Muslim world, *sharia* tends to be confined to family law. Had a second question been asked: 'Do you know of any reputable Muslim legal scholar in Britain who teaches, as a matter of course, that "apostasy laws" should be practised in a non-Muslim state?', the answer again might have been very different!

Notes

1. R. Omaar, *Only Half of Me: Being a Muslim in Britain* (London: Viking, 2006), p. 19.

2. M. Y. Alam (ed.), *Made in Bradford* (Pontefract: Route, 2006), p. 211.

3. A. Sen, *Identity and Violence: The Illusion of Destiny* (London: Penguin, 2006), p. 20.

4. Omaar, *Only Half of Me*, p. 37.

5. See S. H. Nasr, *The Heart of Islam: Enduring Values for Humanity* (New York: HarperSanFrancisco, 2004), pp. 87–100. There are also, of course, Muslim minorities in a range of other cultures, such as China.

6. *The Economist*, 24 July 2006.

7. T. Kucukan, *Politics of Ethnicity, Identity and Religion: Turkish Muslims in Britain* (Aldershot: Ashgate, 1999), p. 63.

8. P. Enneli, T. Modood and H. Bradley, *Young Kurds and Young Turks* (York: Joseph Rowntree Reform Trust, 2005), p. 40.

9. J. Birt and P. Lewis, 'The Pattern of Islamic Reform in Britain: The Deobandis between Intra-Muslim Sectarianism and Engagement with Wider Society', in S. Allievi and M. van Bruinessen (eds), *Producing Islamic Knowledge in Western Europe* (London: Routledge, forthcoming).

10. See M. Q. Zaman, *The Ulama in Contemporary Islam: Custodians of Change* (Princeton: Princeton University Press, 2002) and C. Allen, *God's Terrorists: The Wahhabi Cult and the Hidden Roots of*

Modern Jihad (London: Little, Brown, 2006).

11. It should be noted that Sufis are not pacifist. An American Muslim lists leading Sufis active in nineteenth-century jihad against Western colonial powers in Africa: Nuh Ha Mim Keller's introduction, translation and notes to *Ahmad ibn Naqib al-Misri. Reliance of the Traveller: A Classical Manual of Islamic Sacred Law* (Beltsville, Md: Amana Publications, 1994), p. 863.

12. See R. Eaton, *Essays on Islam and Indian History* (New Delhi: Oxford University Press, 2000).

13. Muslims do not apologize for the early Muslim conquests which created a vast empire from Spain to North India within a hundred years, often referred to in Islamic histories as the 'openings' of the world to Islam. This did not entail the forcible conversion of People of the Book, Christians and Jews, but rather a number of measures indicating their social subordination, even humiliation. See P. Crone, *Medieval Islamic Political Thought* (Edinburgh: Edinburgh University Press, 2004), ch. 21.

14. See Z. Hussain, *The Curry Mile* (London: Suitcase Books, 2006).

15. F. Bodi, 'Beautiful Preaching', *Q-News*, 14–21 April 1995, p. 9.

16. E. Masood, *British Muslims: Media Guide* (London: British Council, 2006), p. 62.

17. C. Peach, 'Islam, Ethnicity and South Asian Religions in the London 2001 Census', *Transactions of the Institute of British Geographers*, n.s. 31 (2006), pp. 354, 364.

18. Ibid., p. 355.

19. Z. Badawi, *Islam in Britain* (London: Ta Ha, 1981), p. 27.

20. S. Z. Abedin, 'Minority Crises, Majority Options', in T. Hashmi and H. Mutalib (eds), *Islam, Muslims and the Modern State* (London: PalgraveMacmillan, 1994), p. 36.

21. E. Moosa, 'Introduction' to F. Rahman, *Revival and Reform in Islam*, ed. E. Moosa (Oxford: Oneworld Publications, 2000), p. 26.

22. Ibid., p. 27. The term 'Orientalism' was popularized by the late Edward Said in a work of that name written in 1978 which argues that oriental scholars have misunderstood the East either out of prejudice or because they have interpreted it through wrong categories, and that their work is too closely aligned with the political interests of their countries and used to justify control and subordination of the colonized. This interpretation has, of course, been subject to sustained critique. See A. Hourani, *Islam in European Thought* (Cambridge: Cambridge University Press, 1991).

23. A. Siddiqui, *Christian–Muslim Dialogue in the Twentieth Century* (London: Macmillan, 1997), p. 196.

24. A. Siddiqui, 'Fifty Years of Christian–Muslim Relations', *Islamochristiana*, 26 (2000), pp. 51–77.

25. T. Abbas, 'British Islam Bounces Back', *Prospect*, 126, web exclusive.

26. R. McGown, *Muslims in the Diaspora: The Somali Communities of London and Toronto* (Toronto: University of Toronto Press, 1999), p. 22.

27. See A. H. Ali, *Infidel: My Life* (London: Free Press, 2007); I. Manji, *The Trouble with Islam: A Wake-Up Call for Honesty and Change* (Edinburgh: Mainstream Publishing, 2004); and A. Wadud, *Inside the Gender Jihad: Women's Reform in Islam* (Oxford: Oneworld Publications, 2006).

28. 'Labour Election Fraud "Would

Disgrace a Banana Republic"', *The Times*, 5 April 2005, pp. 8–9.

29. First broadcast 30 October 2006.

30. W. Schiffauer, 'Migration and Religiousness', in T. Gerholm (ed.), *The New Islamic Presence in Western Europe* (London: Mansell, 1998), p. 147.

31. Ibid.

32. See the survey data published to accompany the Channel 4 *Dispatches* programme about 'Muslim Attitudes to Living in Britain', first broadcast 27 April 2006.

33. Populus poll mentioned in the Policy Exchange report 'Living Apart Together', published 30 January 2007; available from their website, <www.policyexchange.org.uk>.

34. Policy Exchange, 'Living Apart Together', p. 37.

CHAPTER 1

Britain's Muslim Communities: A Sketch

Amir was born in Bolton in 1987. His family's story is in some respects typical of the 70 per cent of British Muslims with roots in South Asia. His grandfather, Lall Khan, came from a small village in Pakistan's Punjab, an hour away from Rawalpindi, a military cantonment. A soldier in the Pakistan army, Lall decided to chance his luck and arrived in the north of England in 1963 with nothing. After picking potatoes in Bradford, he found regular work in a Bolton mill. His wife and four children joined him in 1967. Amir's father was then nine years old.

Before his death, Amir's grandfather had built a solid house in his Pakistani village and a second home in Rawalpindi. Amir's father would also buy a house in Rawalpindi, where he will retire. While dad is at ease in Bolton, for him 'home' remains Pakistan. Not so for Amir. While he enjoys his visits to Pakistan, he describes himself as 'Pakistani in terms of my background, but culturally I'm British, Bolton through and through'. In Pakistan, 'just by the way you stand, walk, your mannerisms, they can tell you are foreign'.[1]

Of course, in other respects Amir is far from typical. In 2005, as a seventeen-year-old, he was catapulted into celebrity status after winning an Olympic silver medal for boxing. His cousin Sajid Mahmood has played cricket for England. After 7/7 Amir found he was being projected as an ambassador of young Britons of Pakistani ancestry. More particularly, he finds that he has metamorphosed from 'Asian lad' to representative 'Muslim'. Amir handles this in his autobiography with humour and characteristic northern common sense.

Amir's family are part of a history of exchange between India and Britain reaching back three hundred years to the founding of the East

India Company, an exchange which saw a growing stream of students, traders and political dissidents in the nineteenth century. A recent history of the Muslim communities in Britain includes an absorbing narrative of a hitherto untold story, that of Muslims in Britain from 1800 to 1945. It is a history enlivened with fascinating portraits of individuals embedded in local Muslim communities: Abdullah Quilliam in Liverpool, appointed Sheikh al-Islam of the British Isles in 1894 by the Ottoman ruler; Abdullah Yusuf Ali, anglophile, Edwardian gentleman, trustee of Woking mosque, a member of that small club of Indians allowed entry to the British establishment, whose translation of and commentary on the Qur'an in 1934 is still available and popular today; Sheikh Abdullah Ali al-Hakimi in Cardiff, who worked among Yemeni and Somali communities. If London was to become a home to Arab radicals in the 1980s and 1990s – leading French academics to label it 'Londonistan' – we learn from this monograph that in the fifty years before the First World War it had become a refuge for Turkish critics of Ottoman tyranny.[2]

Nevertheless, as Amir's story reminds us, substantial Muslim migration only began in the 1950s, to meet a growing labour shortage in the industrial cities of London, the Midlands and the former textile towns of Yorkshire and Lancashire. Britain drew heavily on its ex-colonies, particularly Pakistanis, Bangladeshis, Indians and Turkish Cypriots. The 1962 Commonwealth Immigrants Act, which controlled worker immigration, also permitted family reunification, which unintentionally promoted settled immigration. In the late 1960s there was a further influx of Muslim immigrants amongst the East African Asians expelled with Africanization. In the 1990s there was significant renewed immigration, with East European Muslims fleeing Bosnia and Kosovo, as well as refugees from Afghanistan, Somalia, Turkey and Iraq.

A development cycle for Muslim communities in Britain

It is possible to identify a four-phase development cycle for the majority of Muslim communities settled in Britain, which Amir Khan's family exemplifies: first, the pioneers; then 'chain migration' of generally unskilled male workers from a number of villages; followed by the migration of wives and children; and finally, the emergence of a generation of Muslims born and educated in Britain. The first two stages are clear in Sir Anwar Parvez's 'rags to riches' story, as detailed in the following exchange between him and Navid Akhtar, the producer of a BBC Radio 4 documentary. Parvez's family were farmers who lived in rural Pakistan.

> *Parvez: Mostly there were one to two hundred houses in the village. [Our] village was very small . . . the worst thing was that there was no school there, so we had to walk every day four miles for a middle school education.*
>
> *Akhtar: In 1958, aged 21, he made his way to England and stayed with a cousin in Bradford. There he found work in the woollen mills.*
>
> *Parvez: I was welcomed by everyone [in my* biradari*/clan] . . . they never took any rent or food bill. I got the job so I was totally cared for in every sense.*
>
> *Akhtar: The more you could do for others, the more your status in the* biradari *would grow. In time Sir Anwar left the mills and found a job on the buses. The increase in salary allowed him to pay his own way and to put money aside. He was now in a position to help others.*
>
> *Parvez: I felt my first job was to bring the people here. First I brought my brother-in-law. Then another brother-in-law. Then my own brothers and my uncles . . . Then slowly and steadily I started calling friends as well. So first I looked after my immediate family, then very close friends . . . then I began to look further afield . . . [within my area]. So whenever I called anyone we became two, then two became four [and so on] . . .*
>
> *Akhtar: Like building a chain . . . a network?*
>
> *Parvez: Yes, like a chain. Yes, proudly I can say, I helped my whole area to come here.*
>
> *Akhtar: By the early 1970s he owned a number of supermarkets in central London and was one of the first shopkeepers to open late and seven days a week. Many of the people he had helped to come to Britain now worked for him. Today his company – Best Way Limited – has an annual turnover of one billion pounds . . . In 1999 he was awarded a knighthood in recognition of his charity work.*[3]

Each phase serves to enlarge the range of contacts and familiarity with British society. During the second stage, the intention was for men to work for a few years and return to their country of origin, to be replaced by a relative who could continue sending remittances back. The men often lived in multiple-occupancy flats and houses – one group of textile day workers vacating their beds to be filled with the returning night shift. Most saw no need to develop a good knowledge of the language and culture of their neighbours, sustained as they were by the myth of return.

The third phase is from sojourners to settlers. During this third phase wives join their husbands or a bride is sought from the homeland. With family consolidation, a network of institutions was developed to meet the religious and cultural needs of their families. This typically involved establishing places to worship – initially, a church might extend to them a use of a building, or a couple of houses or redundant commercial buildings would be acquired and converted into a mosque; then an imam would be sought, usually from the homeland, to teach the children the basics of Islam. During this third phase, Muslims had to develop the linguistic and social skills to interface with the municipal authority and key local institutions to make sure service provision was sensitive to their needs, whether in hospital, school or cemetery.

The third and fourth phases, of course, overlap. However, with the emergence of a generation of Muslims born and educated in Britain, more and more Muslims are being incorporated into public and civic society. There has been an increase of Muslim local councillors, to 219 in the UK in 2002 – of which 161 are Labour; an Islamic civil society has emerged, with associations of Muslim lawyers, teachers and doctors; and in centres of high Muslim settlement ethno-religious quarters have been consolidated, with a whole range of goods and services provided by Muslim businessmen and professionals.

Different ethnic communities can be located at different points in this cycle, depending on when they migrated and the circumstances of migration. The Bangladeshis were the last South Asian community to come as economic migrants and they arrived after the collapse of many of the industries which earlier had sought cheap labour, especially textiles. The Somalis are at the bottom of the economic pile, since many only arrived in the 1990s, fleeing civil war.

There is a revealing moment in Rageh Omaar's memoir when he is discussing the costs of going on hajj, the pilgrimage to Mecca, with a Somali travel agent in London. A hierarchy among Muslims has clearly emerged, consisting, on the one hand, of British Asians, mainly from Pakistan and India, who make up the majority of the 27,000

British Muslims who go on hajj every year, along with Arabs and British converts, who can afford to pay the average price of £2,500 to £3,000 per person; and, on the other, the Somalis, Afghans, Yemenis and other Africans. The latter go for a 'supersaver ticket' – all in for £1,300 – since they have no desire to travel on the expensive Emirate or BA flights and stay in three- or four-star accommodation. The travel agent expresses regret that the free market has even affected the hajj.

The changing composition of Muslim communities[4]

The 2001 UK census was the first since 1951 to pose a question about religious identity. Its data indicated that the population of the Muslim communities was 1.6 million, or 2.7 per cent of the UK population. The following offers a partial classification:

1. Sixty-eight per cent (1 million) were of South Asian origin. Pakistanis were the largest group, 43 per cent of all Muslims; Bangladeshis made up 17 per cent and Indians 8 per cent.
2. Twelve per cent described themselves as 'white': about a third of these were 'white British', which includes Turkish Cypriots and white converts. The two-thirds in the 'other white' category consisted of some 60,000 Muslims born in Eastern Europe – Bosnia, Albania and Kosovo – and the rest were Turks, Kurds, North Africans and Middle Easterners.[5]
3. Seven per cent were Black African Muslims. The census tables did not disaggregate their national origins but there were some 7,500 Nigerian-born Muslims, with a further 11,000 from 'other Central and Western African countries'. The remaining component includes a substantial Somali group, with 42,548 born in Somalia.

Until 1981 probably 80 per cent of British Muslims came from South Asia. This has changed in the last decade or so, with an increase due to the arrival of refugees and asylum-seekers. Afghanistan, Iraq and Somalia have all been among the main countries of origin of asylum-seekers for the last few years.

To sum up, the Muslim population in the UK has grown in half a century from 21,000 to 1.6 million. The rate of growth is rapid and the population is young so continued growth is expected, not least because Pakistani and Bangladeshi households are almost twice the size of those of the white majority. Muslims have the youngest age structure of all religious communities. One-third are aged 0–15 compared to an average for the whole population of 20 per cent. Only 6 per cent are aged over 60 compared with 21 per cent for the population as a whole. Demographic projection is an imprecise science but the 2001 population figure for Muslims is likely to double by 2021, to around 3 million.

Since 'Arabs' feature in the popular imagination when the term 'Muslim' is used, one surprise from the data is the relative paucity of Muslims from North Africa and the Arab world – most of whom describe themselves as 'other white' in the 2001 census. Of these, 36,000 were born in North Africa and 93,000 in the Middle East. As yet, it is not possible to disaggregate this figure into ethnicity, place of birth or religion. An earlier study of Egyptians in Britain pointed out that a percentage of them were Coptic Christians and indicated that half of 'Arabs' lived in London. The Egyptians were the largest group and numbered more than 20,000, followed by Iraqis, with 15,000, and Moroccans and Lebanese less than 10,000 each. With the exception of Libyans, who numbered 6,000, all the other communities, including Saudis and Algerians, numbered less than 4,000 each.

While such groups as Saudis resident in the UK are relatively small, Saudi visitors exceed those of all other Arab countries put together. In 2000 there were some 63,000 Saudi visitors. Many are part of a cosmopolitan Arab elite sometimes referred to as 'the Shaykhs of Knightsbridge'.[6] Saudi religious influence in Britain has been inflated by petrodollars. Further, because Saudis and Egyptians dominate Al Qaeda's leadership, Arabs have assumed an exaggerated importance in the media due to security concerns.

In reality, most Arabs in London are international commuters, well-educated students who have chosen to stay, or political exiles whose focus of engagement remains their home country, e.g. Islamists such as the Tunisian Rashid al-Ghannushi. The 'Arabs' in London tend to be much more 'secular' than their South Asian co-religionists. The small Egyptian community encompasses some 1,400 doctors, as well as an elite of several thousand professionals, bankers, academics, businessmen and financiers. Many work for the burgeoning Arabic press in London and for London-based Arabic TV stations. This fact is obscured by the publicity given to high-profile extremists such as the Egyptian Abu Hamza al-Masri, who took over Finsbury Park mosque in London and who was jailed in February 2006 for seven years for soliciting murder and inciting racial hatred.

Geographical distribution

Muslims are highly concentrated in a small number of large conurbations: London (607,000); West Midland Metropolitan County, which includes Birmingham (192,000); Greater Manchester (125,219); and West Yorkshire Metropolitan County, the Bradford-Leeds urban area (150,000). These four areas account for 70 per cent of all Muslims in England and Wales. By contrast, Scotland has 43,000 Muslims, well over 80 per cent of whom have origins in Pakistan, and Northern Ireland less than 2,000.

Table 1 gives the local authorities in England and Wales with the highest percentage of Muslims.[7] Ten of the twenty local authorities with the largest numbers and highest proportions of Muslims in England and Wales are London boroughs. Tower Hamlets, in the East End of London, has the highest percentage of Muslims of all local authorities in the UK and is the third largest after Birmingham and Bradford.

As remarked earlier, the spatial distribution of London's Muslims makes it clear that there are high levels of intra-Muslim ethnic segregation. Bangladeshis, the largest Muslim ethnic group, are highly encapsulated, showing little residential mixing with other groups. White Muslims and Black Caribbean Muslims are separated from

Table 1. Local authorities with the highest percentage of Muslims

Local authority	Number of Muslims	Percentage of overall population
Tower Hamlets	71,389	36.4
Newham	59,293	24.3
Blackburn with Darwen	26,674	19.4
Bradford	75,188	16.1
Waltham Forest	32,902	15.1
Luton	26,963	14.6
Birmingham	140,033	14.3
Hackney	27,908	13.8
Pendle	11,988	13.4
Slough	15,897	13.4

both Indian and Pakistani Muslim communities. Thus emotional attachment to the notion of belonging to a shared Muslim world – the *umma* – fitfully expressed at the time of pilgrimage to Mecca or in opposition to Western foreign policy, does not transcend residential segregation or marriage within ethnically bounded groups.

The study of Egyptians in Britain, though somewhat dated, also pointed out that there is no such thing as an 'Arab community' in Britain:

> *Although Egyptians do not live in physical ghettos, unlike Moroccans in North Kensington or Somalis in London's East End, yet they and other Arab groups inhabit a cultural and social ghetto . . . they do not participate in British public life . . . [and] know more about what goes on in the Arab world than in their own local borough . . . the Egyptians are very different from the Moroccans, the Somalis, the Yemenis and the Iraqis and none of them identifies with the other as part of one community.*[8]

The fact that well over 90 per cent of marriages of British Muslim women from South Asian backgrounds are to co-ethnics can be a source of resentment. One of the respondents in a study of converts to Islam commented bitterly:

> *I think the main problem I have as a new Muslim is the almost complete lack of support I have felt from the Muslim community. They are glad you became a Muslim, but would not invite you to their home, and would not consider marrying an 'English' person – or else they see you as an interesting 'exotic' showpiece.*[9]

Among British Pakistanis, marriage is not only within the same ethnic group, but consanguineous – arranged with relatives – according to clan and caste hierarchies.[10] In a recent study of the Pakistani communities in Oxford, 71 per cent of the 70 marriages studied were transcontinental, with a relative from Pakistan.[11]

What is surprising is that evidence suggests that within certain groups of British Pakistanis, the rate of first-cousin marriage has increased across generations rather than declined. Further, the category 'Pakistani' encompasses distinct regional and linguistic groups: Pathans distinguish themselves from Punjabis, with young Mirpuris – a group to which some two-thirds of all British Pakistanis belong – re-categorizing themselves as 'ethnic Kashmiris' to distance themselves from Pakistanis. A focus on 'religious' commonalities obscures the fact that across Europe, ethnic groups suppressed in their home country are free to organize themselves and assert their political and cultural identity; so among 'Algerians' in France, the Berbers are free to develop separate associations, and the same is true of the Kurds among 'Turks' in Germany. Likewise, among the 'Pakistanis' the Kashmiris are developing a discrete identity.[12] Indeed, in Birmingham a handful of local councillors have been voted in on the back of a discrete Kashmiri political party!

In such a complex context of ethnicity and caste, marriage is often seen as the chosen mechanism to consolidate *biradari* loyalties. In a subsequent chapter we will see that sections of the younger generation are increasingly restive about such transcontinental arranged marriages, especially daughters, who have less freedom to negotiate than sons.

A tale of three cities

While many British Muslim communities are languishing at the base of the economic pyramid, there are significant inter- and intra-ethnic differences. Different economic trajectories depend on a number of variables: pre-migration histories, educational and class profiles, whether migrating communities were urban or rural, and the opportunities and constraints of the different urban contexts in which they find themselves. A good way to illustrate this is to consider Muslim communities in three cities.

Brent

Brent, according to the 2001 census, is the most ethnically diverse local authority in Britain. The 11 per cent of the borough which describes itself in the census as 'Muslim' includes people from at least 25 nationalities. Brent attracts both the upwardly mobile – Bangladeshi unemployment levels in Tower Hamlets are four times those in Brent – and acts as a magnet for asylum-seekers.

The juxtaposition of such ethnic variety has generated enormous energy and creativity. Brent saw the creation of the first state-funded Muslim school and has a Shi'ite Islamic College for Advanced Studies, which offers secondary education and degree courses. It is also the location of a pioneer women's society – An-Nisa – founded in 1985 to gain recognition for Muslim needs in social services, as well as 'sponsoring and organizing cultural events that are reflective of the wider Muslim world'.[13]

The borough is the publishing centre of the most innovative English-speaking Muslim magazine – the monthly *Q-News* – which has been in existence for some fifteen years. *Q-News* seeks to educate and entertain, while contributing to identity-building by facilitating debate across diverse ethnic and sectarian communities. There is also a plethora of organizations which have sought to marry traditional Western concerns with an Islamic ethos, such as the Islamic Human Rights Commission, set up in 1997, and Muslim charities, including Islamic Relief and Muslim Aid.

Leicester

In contrast to Brent, Leicester's Muslim communities are nothing like as diverse. However, they too have a quite distinct profile. The majority are Gujarati Indians, who were forced out of East Africa and Uganda with 'Africanization' in the late 1960s and early 1970s. They arrived with entrepreneurial skills and a good education, which enabled them to adapt easily to and enrich the local economy, which was diverse and buoyant. Initially, they were settled in inner-city areas and did not compete with the indigenous working class for housing, thereby avoiding a possible source of friction.

As 'twice migrants', they had already developed skills to live as a minority, were English-speaking and had little nostalgia for 'home'. Moreover, they were grateful for entry into the UK after the trauma of their expulsion. Good links had already been forged in East Africa and Uganda between the Hindus, now some 15 per cent of Leicester's population, the Sikhs and Muslims. By 2001, the Muslim communities had grown over a twenty-year period from 4 to 11 per cent of the city's total.

While Leicester is often held up as a model of cohesion and positive multiculturalism, a recent study points out that, in reality, there is minimal inter-cultural contact; parallel communities exist as a matter of choice, and a number of political and demographic changes could render relations increasingly difficult. Labour's political dominance, which began in 1979, in part turned on developing a pattern of patron–client politics, with elders in all communities who could consolidate 'ethnic vote-banks'.[14]

Labour's dominance was lost in 2003 when many Muslim voters shifted from Labour to the Liberal Democrats as a protest against the Iraq war. Further, Labour's policy of providing resources for 'diversity' was perceived to be at the expense of addressing deprivation in white working-class areas, some of the most deprived in the country, where its support slumped. The dramatic growth in Muslim communities has come from elsewhere in the country, from asylum-seekers and Europe. In the last few years more than 10,000 Somalis have settled in Leicester, most coming from the Netherlands. Thus, the good working relations between Hindu, Muslim and Sikh elders developed in East Africa can no longer be taken for granted in a new context, a set of Muslim communities with very different histories, whose demographic growth threatens the numerical dominance of the Hindus.

Bradford

Further north, Bradford has a very different story to tell. Leicester's success in incorporating its Muslim communities turned, in large part, on the entrepreneurial and educational skills its English-speaking communities brought with them from East Africa, which readily transferred into an economy marked by diversity and growth. Bradford, like some other northern cities, was too dependent on one major industry, textiles. When this collapsed – 60,000 textile jobs, or 80 per cent of the total, were lost between 1960 and 1990 – the economic niche for the majority of the city's first-generation Muslim migrants in the late 1950s and early 1960s was also removed.

Unlike the East African Gujarati migrants in Leicester, the majority of Muslims in Bradford have roots in rural areas. A large majority of the city's 75,000 Muslims have origins in Pakistan, more particularly Mirpur in Azad Kashmir, a mountainous region and one of the least developed. There are also smaller communities of Bangladeshis with roots in rural Sylhet. Further, while some 16 per cent of the district's population in the 2001 census describe themselves as 'Muslim', the number in school is almost double that figure, due to the age profile of the community.

Given the dramatic decline of the city's main industry, its economic future, in part, depends on being able to attract increased investment to generate more jobs locally and to be able to benefit from regional growth, especially in neighbouring Leeds. The former has begun to happen but has taken longer than hoped because of the negative image of the city created by high-profile crises: whether the 'Rushdie Affair' in 1989, when the city became the epicentre of protests against the novel *The Satanic Verses*, which was publicly burned, or two major riots, one in 1995 and the other in 2001, both with a majority of young local men of Pakistani ethnicity. Further, if local youngsters are to benefit, a great deal depends on the success of the local educational authority, since life skills and a good education are the precondition for access to such jobs as are available.

With regard to educational achievement, the city has a mountain to climb. National and local figures for the Pakistani communities indicate the scale of the challenge. In 1999, nationally, 22 per cent of Pakistani boys achieved five or more GCSEs (grades A* to C), compared to 37 per cent of girls. The equivalent figure for white boys and girls was 45 and 55 per cent respectively (for Indians the figures were even better, 54 and 66 per cent). If these figures were not worrying enough, the Bradford statistics for Pakistani boys and girls were truly disturbing: 17 and 28 per cent. In 2004 the respective national figures for Pakistani boys and girls were 29 and 39 per cent. This was a welcome improvement, if still behind the national average.

In Bradford, there has also been some overall improvement. However, once again the picture is variable. If we analyse some 27 secondary schools, including the ten secondary schools with a majority of South Asian Muslim students – six of which have at least an 85 per cent Muslim intake – four had results still hovering around 20 per cent; four between 30 and 37 per cent and only two schools above 40 per cent, which we might designate average or good. In the 17 secondary schools with a majority white intake, four were also in the first category, only one in the second and 13 were average to good. Probably 10 per cent of the pupils in this last category of school – as well as the city's private schools – are 'Muslims' from South Asian communities. This sector continues to generate the city's successful business and professional community, which includes a growing 'Muslim' presence.

Clearly, the biggest challenge is to raise the level of achievement in the city's eight schools – half of which have a majority white intake, the other half an Asian Muslim majority – whose results could easily translate into an educational underclass. Further, another four schools with an Asian Muslim majority could either topple into the bottom category or move towards the average category. Bradford has long had a troubling minority of white working-class pupils who leave school with very little. The danger is that the city has a growing Asian Muslim school population which threatens to enlarge that sector significantly.

Socio-economic profile of the Muslim communities

It will be clear now that aggregate data about the Muslim population is likely to obscure as much as illuminate. We would expect that newly formed communities of asylum-seekers fleeing violence will share all the disadvantages of any migrant community. However well educated in their home country, unless they have good English they will start at the bottom of the socio-economic pyramid. Those that have fled failed states such as Afghanistan and Somalia will often arrive traumatized. Further, given that the largest Muslim communities, from Pakistan and Bangladesh, are often only one generation removed from rural peasantry, it will take time for these communities to develop the skills and confidence to relate to wider society – as exemplified in the experiences of migrants from rural Turkey to Germany touched on in the previous chapter.

Necessarily, these communities will colour generalized data. However, such statistics ignore the impact of Arab wealth and influence in Britain. In an address delivered to a British Council conference held in London in April 1999 – 'Mutualities: Britain and Islam' – it was pointed out that Britain had benefited enormously from the oil boom of the last twenty years:

> *Petrol dollar surpluses [have found] safe havens in British funds ... some thirty-six Arab banks operate in London alongside more than a hundred Muslim-owned financial institutions ... [most hold] their gold reserves in the Bank of England. Analysts believed that the real estate held by Muslim investors in London property in 1998 and the first quarter of 1999 amounted to well over twenty per cent of the market.*[15]

Nevertheless, generalized data about Muslim communities do indicate worrying trends. One-third of the Muslim population is in either the long-term unemployed or 'never worked' category; this is twice the figure for 'Christian' communities. The main reason for this low Muslim participation in the formal labour force is the absence of Muslim women. Some 70 per cent of Muslim women aged 25 and over were economically inactive in 2001; this compares with less than 30 per cent for Christian women and 35 per cent for Hindus and Sikhs.[16] Moreover, over 40 per cent of this category were classified as 'looking after home/family' – this compares with 13 per cent for the population as a whole. Such low levels of participation often turn on traditional views of *purdah* – a need to 'curtain' women away from non-related Muslims, especially in a Western society routinely dismissed as Godless, and marked by drunkenness, sexual promiscuity and lack of respect for elders.[17]

Although Muslim women are absent from the official labour market, there is a good deal of low-paid home working. Further, there is evidence of increasing polarization within Muslim communities based on class and educational success. Among Pakistani and Bangladeshi women with A levels or degrees the proportion in the labour market appeared higher than many other ethnic groups. Location also matters. The 1991 census data suggested that for Bangladeshis in Brent unemployment rates were some 12 per cent, while in Tower Hamlets it was almost four times that figure. Ethnicity, education and distinct cultural attitudes to gender also explain differences in economic trajectories. Not only was a higher proportion of men from the Middle Eastern, predominantly Muslim, groups more economically active than white males, but the percentage of economically participating females from this group was higher than their white counterparts.[18]

In both the 16–24 and 25–39 age groups, the unemployment rates among the UK Pakistani and Bangladeshi ethnic groups were twice as high as those of the white British men. There are, of course, different rates of unemployment which turn on the length of settlement and the different social capital possessed by different ethnic groups. Thus, the Indian Muslim level of unemployment for men is 11 per cent, while for Black African Muslim men it is 28 per cent. Certain ethnic groups also work in particular industries. One in six Pakistani men were cab drivers or chauffeurs, compared with one in a hundred white British men. One-third of Bangladeshi men were either cooks or waiters, compared with one in a hundred white British men.

Poor educational qualifications and jobs, along with the low percentage of economic activity, leads to an unfavourable tenure pattern in housing. Muslims have the lowest proportion of owner occupation and the highest dependence on social housing of all faith groups. However, if the picture is disaggregated it is far worse for Bangladeshi households, with 48 per cent in social housing compared to only 16 per cent for Pakistanis. It is likely that asylum-seekers (Somalis, Kurds and Bosnians) are also in social housing or private rented accommodation.

The youthful age structure and large family size ensures the rapid growth of certain Muslim communities, especially from South Asia.

These communities, characterized by generally low educational qualifications, and occupational concentrations in restaurants and taxi-driving, offer limited opportunities for progress. Along with low participation of women in the formal labour market and marriage at an early age – which contributes to fewer years of education, lower educational skills and large average family and household size – these factors cumulatively begin to explain the extraordinarily high concentration of Muslims in areas of multiple deprivation. Some 55 per cent of Muslims in England live in areas containing the most deprived housing conditions home to 20 per cent of the total population.[19]

The public profile of Islam and Muslim communities in Britain is likely to be shaped less by sophisticated Muslim professional groups in London or Manchester than by what happens in those cities with young, growing Muslim communities, such as Birmingham, Bradford and Burnley, where Islam has a largely Pakistani face. The Pakistani communities, especially the majority with roots in Kashmir, include a growing underclass with a significant section of young men under-achieving in schools, joining an intractable white underclass on the outer estates. This is also happening with sections of the Bangladeshi and Somali communities.

The 7 July 2001 riots in Bradford, which left more than 300 police officers injured and many citizens traumatized, and caused an estimated £7.5 million damage, involved a majority of young men of South Asian, particularly Pakistani, ethnicity – over 90 per cent of the rioters belonged to this category. Almost 200 people were subsequently sentenced – many having been handed over to the police by parents and relatives. 'A clear majority of the offenders were previously known to the police (62%) and almost 60% of the non-student offenders were unemployed.'[20]

Such riots, along with serious disturbances in the same period in Oldham and Burnley, open the door to extremists in both communities intent on capitalizing on a widespread feeling of malaise, whether the British National Party (BNP) or Hizb ut-Tahrir ('Party of Liberation') – a radical Islamist group with roots in Palestine, dubbed by Muslim and non-Muslim alike as the Islamic BNP, given its supremacist and exclusionary rhetoric. We will explore the dynamics, influence and appeal of such radical Islamist groups in a later chapter.

Notes

1. A. Khan with K. Garside, *Amir Khan, a Boy from Bolton: My Story* (London: Bloomsbury, 2006), pp. 81–2.

2. See H. Ansari, *The Infidel Within: Muslims in Britain since 1800* (London: Hurst and Co., 2004).

3. 'The *Biradari*', BBC Radio 4, first broadcast 26 August 2003.

4. For the data in this section I have drawn on two seminal articles by the social geographer C. Peach: 'Islam, Ethnicity and South Asian Religions in the London 2001 Census', *Transactions of the Institute of British Geographers*, n.s. 31 (2006), pp. 353–70, and 'Muslims in the 2001 Census of England and Wales: Gender and Economic Disadvantage', *Ethnic and Racial Studies*, 29 (2006), pp. 629–55.

5. The figures for converts usually mentioned in the literature range between five and ten thousand; see A. Adnan, *New Muslims in Britain* (London: Ta Ha, 1999).

6. M. Al-Rasheed, 'Saudi Religious Transnationalism in London', in M. Al-Rasheed (ed.), *Transnational Connections and the Arab Gulf* (London: Routledge, 2005), p. 153.

7. I have borrowed this table from D. Hussain, 'The Impact of 9/11 on British Muslim Identity', in R. Geaves, T. Gabriel, Y. Haddad and J. Idleman Smith (eds), *Islam and the West, Post 9/11* (Aldershot: Ashgate, 2004), p. 118.

8. G. Karmi, *The Egyptians of Britain: A Migrant Community in Transition*, CMEIS Occasional Paper 157 (Durham: University of Durham, Centre for Middle Eastern and Islamic Studies, 1997), p. 25. This study focuses largely on the first generation of migrants. It would be useful to have an update exploring whether and to what extent the situation has changed with regard to their children.

9. Adnan, *New Muslims in Britain*, p. 33.

10. As noted in Chapter 1, the term for clan is *biradari*, 'brotherhood', an extended kinship group, sometimes also referred to as *zats* or castes, which are organized hierarchically: at the top are the respectable castes – *ashraf* – which claim descent from the Prophet or the Prophet's tribe, Muslim rulers, or Afghan invaders; then the land-owning castes – *zamindar* – and at the bottom of the pyramid, the artisan castes – *kami*.

11. A. Shaw, 'Kinship, Cultural Preference and Immigration: Consanguineous Marriage among British Pakistanis', *Journal of the Royal Anthropological Institute*, n.s. 7 (2001), p. 327.

12. See P. Ellis and Z. Khan, 'Diasporic Mobilisation and the Kashmir Issue in British Politics', *Journal of Ethnic and Migration Studies*, 24 (1998), pp. 471–88.

13. S. Ameli, *Globalization, Americanization and British Muslim Identity* (London: Islamic College for Advanced Studies Press, 2002), p. 122.

14. G. Singh, 'A City of Surprises: Urban Multiculturalism and the "Leicester model"', in N. Ali, V. S. Kalra and S. Sayyid (eds), *A Postcolonial People: South Asians in Britain* (London: Hurst and Co., 2006), p. 299.

15. British Council, *Mutualities: Britain and Islam* (London: British Council, 1999), n. p.

16. T. Choudhury, *Muslims in the UK: Policies for Engaged Citizens* (New York: Open Society Institute, 2005), p. 211.

17. Peach, 'Muslims in the 2001 Census', p. 645.

18. Ansari, *The Infidel Within*, p. 191.

19. Peach, 'Muslims in the 2001 Census', p. 650.

20. A. Carling, 'Bradford's Programme for a Peaceful City: An Experiment in Theory and Practice', in S. Smith (ed.), *Applying Theory to Policy and Practice* (Aldershot: Ashgate, forthcoming). I am grateful to Dr Carling for allowing me to read his chapter before publication.

CHAPTER 2

Mind the Gap: Understanding Inter-generational Tensions

In the UK population at large one in five are under 16 and one in six over 65. In the Muslim communities the figures are one in three and 1 in 25 respectively. In short, more than half a million Muslim youngsters are under 16. In an ageing population, this should be an important resource. However, all is not well. Shareefa Fulat, the director of the Muslim Youth Helpline, worries about a potential social crisis, exacerbated by a shortage of mainstream youth provision sensitive to faith and culture. She remarks that

> *The problems faced by Muslim youth are similar to their non-Muslim peers: drugs, mental health, relationships, careers, jobs training and sexuality. For the Muslim community, most of these issues are considered taboo or are largely ignored, making the problems more acute for young Muslims. Any recognition of these issues is largely in the form of chastisement and judgmentalism. In addition, the identity and lifestyle conflicts experienced by many Muslims ... may mean that far from providing any support, the family or community are the source of the problem.*[1]

Inter-generational tensions are part of growing up. This chapter will seek to understand why such tensions are particularly acute in sections of the Muslim community. The focus will be on the British community with roots in Pakistan and Kashmir, since they are easily the largest set of Muslim communities in Britain and, unsurprisingly, shape the public profile of Muslim communities in many parts of the country.

The novelist and the Sufi

A novel and an address delivered by a Sufi invited to speak to youngsters in Bradford can cast light on the context and challenges facing many young Muslims brought up in the often harsh world of Britain's inner cities.

M. Y. Alam is one of a number of young writers awarded £7,000 by the Arts Council in 2003 for demonstrating 'exceptional promise'. He won the award for his second published work, a crime novel set in Bradford, his home town, entitled *Kilo*. In an interview given to the local press, he expressed the view that

> Kilo *is relevant to people who don't normally pick up a novel. My nephew read it, he's 15, and he watches films. He read it in three days and thought it was great. He was engaged by the reality of it ... I think that [it] ... has things in it relevant to younger people in Bradford ... I hate the idea of being a role model ... how many Bradford-born Pakistani writers are there? When I was growing up there was no-one I could relate to.*[2]

Whatever its literary merit, *Kilo* is no Harry Potter tale. The main character is Khalil Khan, nicknamed 'Kilo', the son of a shopkeeper. The novel opens with his father's humiliation as he is unable to protect Kilo from violence inflicted on them both by two protection racketeers, 'Charlie Boy' and 'Pony Tail'. Kilo gradually loses respect for his father, who in his troubles drinks his profits away. Kilo leaves home and his metamorphosis from a polite young man into the streetwise, gun-toting, knife-wielding drug dealer begins. However, he has a bad conscience and the intervention of a good cop and a religious epiphany returns him to the straight and narrow. The novel is no apologia for drugs – indeed, its unvarnished depiction of the moral and social disintegration of many involved in the drug trade has led youth workers to use it for anti-drug training among young men at risk.

The novel is full of sharp comments about a number of controversial issues. First is the widespread phenomenon of transcontinental arranged marriages, Kilo's refusal of which leads to his father throwing him out:

> *Thing is, that girl from Pakistan probably didn't want to know me at all. Two people, her and me both, were being squeezed here. In all likelihood, she hated the idea of marrying a stranger possessing*

some strange culture as much as I did. That's what it came down to, this cross fertilisation of people, this bridging of the culture gap by force. I could imagine her parents trying to force me on her, and while I had the liberty to bitch about it, she'd be sitting there, head bowed, ready to accept it, silently praying for a husband who treated her okay.[3]

Second is the outwardly pious fathers who know how their sons earn a living pushing drugs but prefer to enjoy the fruits of this rather than challenge it:

These days I see fathers, five-times-a-day people with beards, the prayer beads and the ticket to Paradise, knowing damn well what their sons are up to and not doing a thing about it. Matter of fact, as long as the sons bring a few hundred notes every week to go towards the mansions in Pakistan, or the upkeep of the family four wheel drive, there's no problem. When money comes into it, conflicts between religious beliefs and criminal activities are suddenly and quite miraculously overcome.[4]

When a policeman accuses him of killing his own people by pushing drugs, he responds angrily:

Me killing people? My people? . . . had someone just made me non-elected leader . . . without having the decency to have asked me first? I had no people, *I didn't claim to be a politician, nor did I push myself as one of those selfish bastards who claimed to lead the community.*[5]

Finally, there are bitter comments about rote learning at the mosque which has no impact on the behaviour of young men:

I never understood any of it [the Qur'an] as a kid. I'd go to mosque, read a few pages and then I'd go home like all the other kids. Like them, I knew how to read, how to pronounce, where to pause and where not to, but I never understood like I should have understood. Just a load of words in Arabic, could have been Russian, for all the difference it made . . . I could have been a monkey, mimicking and learning by rote, being conditioned into reading for the sake of it but not for the sake *of it.*[6]

Significantly, Kilo's rehabilitation involves access to the Qur'an, but this time in English, which is able to touch his soul.

As a good novelist, Alam writes about people and communities, warts and all. This includes criminality, with which elders can collude or about which they are in denial. Such novels are not works of social science – although Alam happens to teach that subject in Bradford University! – but nonetheless indicate that British-born writers are contributing to an understanding of 'Muslim' communities which neither idealizes nor demonizes them.

Charlie Boy's casual racism and brutality is clear, yet his obnoxious sidekick, Pony Tail, is a Pakistani. The unvarnished portrayal of Kilo's father, working long hours, harried by criminals and turning to alcohol, has the ring of truth. Such insights challenge the easy dichotomy with which policy-makers often operate: elder/conformist versus youth/deviant. Empirical study of the British Pakistani community soon dispels the myth of the first generation as a completely law-abiding and conformist group. After all, many were a long way from home and exposed to enforced celibacy; some succumbed to the temptations of alcohol and extramarital affairs; a few engaged in benefit fraud. To argue otherwise is a form of 'historical amnesia'.[7]

The world of *Kilo* was also the context of an address delivered in February 2003 by an American Sufi, Shaikh Hamza Yusuf, who spoke in English to some four to five thousand young people in a large Bradford mosque.[8] It was clear from the introductory remarks by a local doctor about a rising drug and substance abuse problem in the community that this was not going to be an occasion to evade difficult contemporary issues.

It was clear from Hamza Yusuf's presentation that he was a scholar of Arabic and the traditional Islamic sciences. He also was able to draw on a wide set of references outside Islam, including Chinese wisdom and Thomas Hobbes, the seventeenth-century English political philosopher. The shaikh began by commending the sign-language facility for the deaf as a welcome development within a community which often neglected this group. He then sought to put the present crisis facing the Muslim world in a historical and spiritual context. He rehearsed familiar 'stages' in the spiritual life which the believer touched by Sufism – Islam's experiential and interior dimension – was called to traverse: the first, repentance; the second, patience, not least in the face of tribulation.

He went on to recall Islam's historic presence in Britain. In the sixteenth and seventeenth centuries some Britons had chosen to become Muslims, since the Ottoman world was much more of a meritocracy and was also characterized by greater tolerance than England at that time. Islam's historic vocation had been a civilizing one – indeed, he argued that the same word in Arabic was used for colonization and civilization. Speaking post-9/11, he pointedly noted that 'We [Muslims] can only be a civilizing presence if we ourselves are not barbarians!'

Hamza Yusuf reminded his audience that Islamic history and religious traditions encompassed two essential prerequisites for human rights: human dignity and equality. The Jewish historian Bernard Lewis was cited as acknowledging that traditionally Jews in the Muslim world had greater security than those in the pre-modern West. In the light of such comments he could address those angry voices in the Muslim world who argued for the forcible expulsion of all Jews from the entirety of Israel/Palestine. He insisted that the Muslim case against them is neither religious nor racist – anti-Semitic – but political: an opposition to a Zionist ideology which sought to justify an illegitimate authority exercised over occupied territories, an occupation enabled and supported by the USA. While accepting the legitimacy of the Palestinian struggle – within legal and ethical norms – he tried to undercut the 'contempt and disdain' some Muslims show for Jews and Christians, too readily and inaccurately dismissed as *kuffar* (infidels).

Turning to the rising drug problem in the Muslim community, he counselled the need for compassion for users. 'Why the flight to oblivion?' What had gone wrong in families, communities and society? He asked provocatively: 'Why do we internalize in our family life the very political despotism from which we have fled in our homelands?' The mark of any society's health is its ethics. 'We have failed to inculcate sound ethics in our children'. In Islam rights to property and life are sacred. Hence his dismay at the riots in Bradford in 1995 and 2001. At the same time, he made some criticisms of corporate capitalism, which exploits child labour in South Asia to provide cheap products. He had a clever aside about USA policy: it used to be said that Britain 'rules the waves'; the USA 'waives the rules'!

His remarks on religious diversity were particularly pertinent. He argued that the Qur'an acknowledges religious diversity as a given. The implication was that it was not God's will for all to be Muslims. He pointed out that some Islamic schools of law had embodied this understanding in extending the traditional protection afforded to the 'People of the Book' – Christians and Jews – to other religious traditions. The shaikh also made space for Muslims to learn from others. He cited the importance the Catholic Church gave to pre-marriage guidance. This would be useful for Muslims to emulate as an antidote to the increase in dysfunctional families. Equally, the West could learn from Islam, which, as the historian Arnold Toynbee had noted, had been more successful in addressing racism and alcoholism.

The shaikh worried about rising sectarianism within the Muslim communities, often fuelled by ignorance masquerading as learning. He reminded his listeners that those who were serious scholars knew that Islamic jurisprudence acknowledged a place for valid disagreements on a range of issues. Further, he expressed dismay at how Qur'anic verses were often being torn out of context, e.g. 'Kill the polytheists wherever you come across them' (cited from an Afghan video) or 'Do not take Jews and Christians as friends' (cited from the radical group Hizb ut-Tahrir). While offering his own more eirenic exegesis, he expressed concern at the damage done by a proliferation of self-taught 'fools' – those issuing legal opinions without adequate training.

He cautioned against for ever looking for external causes for troubles within the Muslim community. 'We are weak and divided'. Sections of the community were locked into 'arrogant argumentation' with each other. In brief, Muslims do not 'embody tranquillity and piety', but are led by 'passions and whims'.

He made some very sharp comments about women's rights. In conditions of social corruption, he argued, it was understandable that religious scholars – *'ulama* – from South Asia had preferred women not to come to the mosque. However, in changed conditions in the West, Muslim leaders should embody the Prophet's teaching and practice, which runs counter to this prohibition. Education, religious and secular, is of vital importance for women, if a new generation of Muslims are to be appropriately schooled.

A question-and-answer session followed his presentation. To the many questions from women he responded by affirming their rights. While Muslim women about to be married were often given a traditional manual on right behaviour – *Bihishti Zewar* (Heavenly Ornaments), written a hundred years earlier in India – where, he demanded, was the equivalent manual for men?[9] Islamic law, he reiterated, was against forced marriage. Verbal abuse, he reminded his listeners – not simply physical abuse by a husband – was a legitimate ground for divorce.

He urged British Muslims to be alert to their many allies in all aspects of life, whether the media, civil service or police. He was concerned that Muslims were alienating the majority society: such alienation was 'foolish, dangerous and giving Islam a bad name'. As to whether Muslims should flee from corrupt, non-Muslim society, he pointed out that there is always a case for leaving a corrupt part of a city for a better part. However, today, with globalization and migration, the medieval notion of a geographically discrete 'House of Islam' locked into endless conflict with an equally discrete 'House of War' was an outmoded theoretical concept. Indeed, some Muslim scholars could speak of Britain/the West as the 'House of Islam'. He asked rhetorically: 'With regard to judicial process in courts where would most people prefer to be tried – in Muslim or Western countries?'

To those who spoke of only obeying God's law – *sharia* – and by implication feeling free to ignore or override British law, he argued that such a position was based on ignorance. From time immemorial the Muslim world had made commercial contracts with the non-Muslim world. This presupposed shared understandings of justice within humanity, approximating to natural law, which clearly did not depend only on *sharia*.

With regard to the vexed status of 'cultural norms' which communities carried with them to the UK, he stated that Islamic law recognized a variety of local customs: a Scottish Muslim could still enjoy haggis, albeit made from *halal* ingredients! Islam, he insisted, came to purify, not obliterate, local custom. Many British Muslims might be ethnically Punjabi but their parents needed to recognize that they were 'culturally British'. They needed to enable youngsters to 'take the best and leave the rest' from both cultures. It was important that parents allowed this process of discernment to take place, otherwise their children would become culturally schizophrenic or be locked into an identity crisis.

This was a masterly presentation. He briefly commented on the situation in the wider Muslim world – especially Israel/Palestine – but resisted the temptation to engage in a sustained indictment of the non-Muslim world, the stock in trade of so many Muslim preachers, which can generate a debilitating sense of victimhood.

In all, the focus of his talk remained a critical and constructive engagement with many of the difficult issues which British Muslims face. What was heartening was that such a large crowd of young people had come to hear him. This suggests a desire for an expansive understanding of Islam which can enable the young to be at ease with their multiple identities: British, Muslim, Pakistani. What was also significant was the presence outside the mosque of a radical Muslim group, so beloved of the national media, Hizb ut-Tahrir, distributing their literature who hardly numbered a dozen!

We will explore in a later chapter the crisis in religious authority to which Hamza Yusuf refers with his remarks about self-styled teachers with a superficial grasp of the Islamic tradition which can wreak havoc, generating a discourse of hate. Here we will reflect on a number of themes common to novelist and religious leader alike: parenting and parental priorities, education – especially the relationship of mosque formation and state school – and leadership at city level, the last of which prompted Kilo's bitter and dismissive comments.

Thwarted dreams?

The educational charity Young Voice produced an insightful study a few years ago with the telling title *Thwarted Dreams: Young Views from Bradford*. It interviewed over 300 young people from 14 to 18, a large majority of whom were from the inner city and from South Asian Muslim communities. This was part of a national study of youth in inner-city areas intended to identify what promotes and what discourages positive attitudes among teenagers and how parents can best help their children to achieve their potential.

What was striking was the number and variety of obstacles to the youngsters – most of whose parents had roots in rural Pakistan – achieving their potential. In comparison with the national data – on youngsters from similar socio-economic backgrounds – only 11 per cent of the local sample, compared to 34 per cent nationally, showed a high level of 'life skills' – skills deemed essential to make the transition to adult life, such as handling money, eating well, dealing with stress, applying for work, making relationships work, and knowing how to find services for young people. Thirty-eight per cent, or three times the national figure, said that their families needed them at home, which influenced their decision either to drop out of education or to choose to study near home.

Many parents were reluctant to allow their daughters to study after 18 or to go away from home. This is partly because the Muslim community is deeply opposed to mixed halls of residence but seems unaware that single-sex provision exists. Similarly, they feared that co-education would mean their daughters would abandon traditional values and turn 'bad' like the Rude Boys, Asian gangs or 'white girls who had babies at twelve'.[10]

A recurring theme was the suffocating impact on the young of community pressure exercised by the extended family embedded in clans, the *biradari*. For fear of being ostracized within their tightly knit community, parents would not allow their child to do something not thought appropriate. This might include the type of subject or course chosen, or the place where it was to be studied. There were also a paucity of good role models within the communities: only 52 per cent had fathers in work, compared to 71 per cent nationwide; only 30 per cent had a mother in work, compared to 65 per cent in the national sample. Since many mothers did not have good English, they seldom had the confidence to attend parents' evenings; others felt excluded from this space because of the presence of men.

Many youngsters were anxious that their communication skills were not adequate. One reason advanced was that boys and young men were required to go to the *madrasa* – mosque school – every day after school for a couple of hours of Islamic teaching, after which they were hurried back home to do homework and then to bed. There was little opportunity for play, sport or socializing together – let alone socializing with non-Muslims. When one adds to that a real fear of bullying and racism, their worlds seem terribly circumscribed. Perhaps it is not surprising that while in the national sample two-thirds believed that they could achieve their goals, less than half of the Bradford sample did.

Youth workers describe how young people who have been overprotected by anxious families cope with going away to college in another town. Either they find the experience liberating, or they are so unprepared for the freedom that they cannot handle it. 'Some feel utterly bewildered, unprepared to manage their own lives ... On returning home they are once again expected to conform and some cannot do this without rebellion or anger or frustration.'[11]

Bridging the gap between school and *madrasa*?

There have been a number of initiatives across the country by local educational authorities (LEAs) to enable schools to engage with parents and *madrasa*, so as to raise the educational achievement of British Pakistani boys. These have been documented in an excellent research report for schools and LEAs which offers helpful advice on how to reduce suspicion between state schools and parents, as well as schools and Islamic 'places of study', the literal meaning of *madrasa*.

The report notes that the staff of a secondary school in Leicester, which serves an economically deprived inner-city area with a majority of Muslim pupils, were surprised to discover that 94 per cent of its year 7 intake attended the mosque. 'Eighty-four per cent went every day throughout the working week and the majority remained there for at least two hours'.[12] The study draws on a range of good practice to enlist parental support and engage with imams in *madrasa*s to work together for the good of the children.

However, there are other issues – a continuing preference for transcontinental marriage, and other cultural, linguistic and religious practices – which need to be factored in and addressed if the raising of standards is to be sustained. A micro-study of an inner-city primary school in a northern city with a majority of British Pakistani pupils offers a window into some of these issues. The study was commissioned by the Children's Society to encourage fathers' involvement in their children's education. The sample of 23 fathers found that most worked as taxi-drivers or in restaurants, which involved long and often anti-social hours. This meant that most were not free to attend after-school meetings; further, the school was seen as the preserve of women, with the mosque as the male preserve. In a tightly knit community, if men were seen moving into this female space, tongues would wag and their motives would be questioned, given the community's preference for *purdah* (gender segregation).

The research found that in every household that took part, with one exception, one parent was a new migrant. Furthermore, 'More than half of the fathers interviewed were not able to communicate in English fluently. Most came to Britain as new migrants to join their wives. The vast majority … were from rural backgrounds.'[13] Two-thirds of wives were unable to read or write English. 'Two thirds of the fathers gave cultural reasons for their lack of involvement in their children's education. These included the mixing of unrelated men and women, the large presence of women, language problems and activities coinciding with mosque [prayer times]'.[14]

The linguistic politics of Pakistan also has an impact on British Pakistanis. The biggest province of Pakistan is the Punjab. However, the national language of Pakistan is not Punjabi, but Urdu – the mother tongue of only 7 per cent of Pakistanis. Urdu is also the vehicle for the teaching of Islam in most of the mosques in Britain that serve the British Pakistani community. The schooling of the

Pakistani urban elite is in English, and they usually insist that their children be taught to read the Qur'an in Arabic, without translation. Writing of this elite, a Pakistani historian wryly remarks that they 'grew up literate not in one language but practically illiterate in at least four'.[15]

In Britain, many Pakistani parents still assume that their children should be exposed to the same four languages. However, unlike the situation in Pakistan, the first language of their children has become English, rather than Punjabi or the Mirpuri variant, Pathwari. For obvious reasons, the children need to have a working knowledge of their parents' mother tongue – especially where one or both parents are more at ease in that language than English. In most mosques, the language of instruction traditionally has been Urdu – the language of high Islamic culture in South Asia, from where the large majority of the religious personnel of the mosque originate, though this is beginning to change with the first cohort of religious scholars trained in Britain finding their way into mosques. Finally, as in Pakistan, a great deal of time in the *madrasa* is devoted to learning the Qur'an in Arabic without translation.

While young British Pakistanis whose parents are both from Mirpur often claim to be multilingual, the reality can be quite different. A recent, localized study indicated that most, when asked to write their name in Urdu or give directions in their Punjabi dialect, were unable to do so. Competence in English was also variable. The vast majority spoke to each other in slang. For the boys influenced by rap or American gangsta music its use was something of which to be proud – less so for girls, given the misogynous lyrics. 'Some intentionally spoke slang while, for others, it was not out of choice but they had missed the opportunity to learn formal or proper English while at school.'[16]

Not only are huge linguistic demands being made of young people, but the pedagogical assumptions of mosque and school are often quite distinct. This important issue has recently been the focus of research by a Muslim scholar who is both a theologian and an educationalist. Dr Sahin's research poses the critical question facing Muslim educators in Britain: what does it mean to be educated Islamically in a multicultural society?

To explore this question, Dr Sahin researched the attitudes of Muslim students, aged 16 to 20, in three sixth-form colleges in inner-city Birmingham. The majority of the students had parents with roots in South Asia. Most of the 400 students questioned had a strong emotional connection with Islam but a significant minority were clear that their understanding of Islam was different from that of their parents.

With regard to personal religiosity, Sahin developed a typology around the twin poles of commitment and exploration. Those with a religious commitment not informed by personal exploration he characterized as 'foreclosed'; those showing little evident interest in religion he dubbed as 'diffuse'; and those searching to make sense of religion he dubbed 'exploratory'.

Those with a diffuse identity believed in the basic teachings of Islam but did not participate in Islamic practice. They lacked personal commitment but wanted to preserve Islam as a cultural element in their lives, an identity marker that enabled them to resist assimilation into what they called 'white culture'. Those with a foreclosed identity viewed Islam in an ahistoric way, presupposing that *sharia* is unchanging and applicable for all times and places. Islam thus understood as a perfect system should not be expected to adapt to changing situations; it is the situations that must adapt to Islam.

Those with a foreclosed identity envisaged an unbridgeable gap between the Islamic community and the rest of society. They expressed the view that they were living in the land of the infidel – *dar al kufr* – deemed morally decadent, contact with whom was to be avoided. They were *in* but not *of* the multicultural society.

The majority, however, embodied an exploratory identity, which, unlike the majority of parents, sought to interpret Islam as relevant to their lives outside home and ethno-religious enclave. There was a strong emphasis on being *British* Muslims. Those with a foreclosed identity tended to be male, while most of the females were in the exploratory and questioning category, in part a response to the greater control to which they were exposed at home and within their communities.

Sahin wisely comments that too many social scientists assume that young Muslims are either victims trapped between two cultures or able to switch effortlessly between cultures. Instead, his research suggests that Muslims feel the need to initiate a meaningful dialogue among the different cultural practices they have internalized. The critical question is whether Muslim educators can engage with such an exploratory impulse. If they cannot, those with an exploratory identity could well become either diffuse or foreclosed.

Sahin worries that traditional Islamic education, with its 'teacher-text centred approach' and emphasis on memorizing a body of knowledge rather than encouraging a critical dialogue between text and context – the complex lived reality – is simply ill equipped to nurture a mature Islamic identity. The consequences are potentially dire:

> *Despite the fact that many British young Muslims speak and think in English, there is not a well-worked-out Qur'anic pedagogy in English. Thus, many of these young people are left either ignorant of this fundamental source of Islam or at the mercy of radical transnational Islamic groups, which try to indoctrinate them into a rigid ahistorical understanding of Islam.*[17]

The other problem, which Sahin does not directly address, is the increasing availability of Islamic texts produced from within the world of traditional South Asian Islam, such as *Bihishti Zewar*, the work noted by Shaikh Hamza Yusuf, translated into English as *Heavenly Ornaments*. This text, written for women by Maulana Ashraf 'Ali Thanwi (d. 1942) – one of the most respected scholars of the influential Deobandi Indian school of thought – is readily accessible in Muslim bookshops and mosques across the country in English translation. It embodies a set of assumptions and ideals for women which cannot but be problematic in twenty-first-century Britain.

A scholarly annotated translation of this work notes that it takes for granted that women are socially subordinate to men. Indeed, religious knowledge is commended for women so as to be better able to 'manage' them. The ideal is for women to remain at home, secluded from all but family and selected female friends. Thanwi 'lists women among men's possessions. Following the *hadis* [*hadith*], he identifies dominant women as a sign of the Last Day ... women [generally] are the greatest number in hell ... A woman is to follow her husband's will and whims in all things, to seek his permission on all issues ... [She] is expected to be responsible for her husband's happiness and to respond to his mood ... "Never think of him as your equal, never let him do any work for you..."'[18]

Clearly, if educational underachievement is to be addressed, religious and cultural factors cannot be ignored. In the past, an anti-racist and class analysis was taken to offer an adequate explanation. While a beginning has been made across a range of Pakistani/Kashmiri communities to discover what sort of educational interventions are making a difference, this is unlikely to be enough. There is a need for serious research to evaluate what cumulative significance such factors as transcontinental marriage, multiple language use, different styles of teaching in school and mosque, as well as poverty and inner-city location, have on education.

However, such discussions can no longer afford to bypass the opinions of young British Muslims themselves. It is no longer enough to allow elders and community gatekeepers to speak for youth – not least because an evident bewilderment among elders about what is happening to sections of their youth translates into a blame culture. Typical of this are the remarks of some Kashmiri elders from Oldham, one of whom summed up a widespread feeling of dismay:

> *The children* vigre ge *(are spoilt). Here ... all they do is sell drugs and thieve ... Another big problem ... is single parents, there are too many of them. We have uneducated parents marrying their daughters and sons to people from Mirpur and then they get divorced. It is the fault of parents that these boys are in such a bad state. They have no responsibility. [The boys] won't go to weddings or to ...* mattam *[mourning rituals] unless forced.*[19]

An elephant in the room

> The Pakistani community in Britain has been established here for over forty years. Now in their third generation they face a crisis which threatens to undermine their future. At the heart of the problem lies the *biradari*, the extended clan network that governs all families and gives values and a sense of identity. Invisible to the outside world, a battle is taking place between *biradari* diehards and those who believe it has no place in modern British society. The youth are the casualties.

With this stark comment, Navid Akhtar, a young British documentary and film maker, begins the second of two programmes on prime-time BBC Radio 4 about the history, changing dynamics, and increasingly negative impact of the *biradari* on all aspects of Pakistani life in Britain.[20] Akhtar visits communities across the country, talking to a range of youth workers, councillors and local radio producers, as well as academics, politicians and young British Pakistanis in Pakistan.

He starts with Rashid's story. Rashid explains that he is a Jat, one of the highest castes – along with Rajputs.

> *Like a royal. Then you have the shoesmiths, the blacksmiths . . . the weavers. Jat means that we own land, that we have people working under us . . . the menial classes. The Jats are more superior in a way. There are more of us. We have more clout. I was born in Bradford. Went to college doing A level law and sociology.*
>
> *After one year [he was 17] my father said: 'Right son. You are going to Pakistan.' I thought I was going for a holiday. No, [I was told,] you are going to get married. I asked him: 'Sorry? Who is she. I do not know her.' He said: 'She is your uncle's daughter; she is good looking; everything is cool.' I got married and came back hoping to restart my education again. But my wife was expecting. So I had to abort my education and start working in a textile mill. I had to do what the family told me to do. To keep the family happy.*

Rashid discovered that his bride was coveted by other relatives within his *biradari*. The gossip machine went into overdrive:

> *They would say at that time – when I was working seven days a week – that he is [only] working five days a week; he has a* gori, *a white girl on the side by whom he has had kids . . . One day, I returned from work; no wife; no food on the table . . . I go to a relative's house and she is there; I tell her not to listen to them because they will mess you up. She says no: they are my uncles so would not mislead . . . Everyone jumped on me, so I just lost it and beat everyone up.*

The marriage ends and Rashid finds himself in prison for grievous bodily harm. Akhtar asks him what he would have done had he carried on studying for his A levels. He replies,

> *My ambition was to get somewhere. A law teacher. But unfortunately things worked out differently. Makes me think. No one asked me this question. In fact, no one has ever asked me that question. It makes me sad, being in England all my life and gaining nothing.*

Akhtar explains that the Pakistani community in Britain is divided into *biradaris* – a system of ancient clans, imported lock, stock and barrel from rural Pakistan, which gives families their identity, a code of behaviour and a support network. For the first generation, as evident in the remarks earlier about Sir Anwar Parvez's rags-to-riches story, it was a resource both enabling migration – drumming up travel costs – and offering essential support when in Britain.

> *Good times, bad times, there is always someone there for you. If you need money someone in the* biradari *will always help you out. When there is a dispute the* biradari *sorts it out. When you die the* biradari *savings account pays to send your body back to Pakistan. It is such an integral part of Pakistani culture but most people do not even think about it, it is just there.*

However, Akhtar cites a chairman of Coventry's Muslim community centre who points out that *biradari* as a resource has become, for many, a constraint – referred to pejoratively as *biradari*-ism – holding the communities back. 'The negative aspects of *biradari*-ism promote "honour" … [insisting] that our clan is better than the other clan which I think is detrimental to the community as a whole.' Rivalries between the two major *biradaris* in Pakistan – the Rajputs, the former land-owners, and the Jats, who farmed the land – are imported into Britain and reignited, 'mostly by men in their sixties who make all the key decisions about running the clan. The blood line must be protected at all costs and the honour of the clan upheld.'

Such attitudes are increasingly resisted by the second and third generations, who have grown up in a liberal society where the emphasis is on individual success and do not want to be held back by a centuries-old tradition. Akhtar points out that 'the fallout of this [inter-generational tension] has been devastating. What was once a hard working, law abiding community seems to have lost its sense of direction. Unemployment is high, educational achievement is low and there is growing concern about high levels of crime and drug addiction.'

Muhammad Bashir is an officer with the West Midlands police force. He has seen the youth problem at first hand:

> *The younger lads – ones who probably do not have the education [or] career prospects – get involved in stealing, burglaries, whatever … they are [often] doing it for the kicks to fit into other groups. By the same token some are getting involved in crime so as to be seen to be successful. For example if someone is unemployed they get involved in crime to finance [having] a nice car, the latest gear … they are out there making an impression to other members of the community saying: 'Look how successful I am.'*

Similarly, drugs is an escalating problem. A youth worker for a project helping drug addicts in Blackburn comments that '*biradari* rivalry fuels the need to appear successful. As many Pakistani communities are in deprived areas some parents will ask no questions so long as the children are bringing in the money' – a point made, as we have seen, in the novel *Kilo*.

Akhtar discovered that hundreds of Pakistani youngsters are being sent back to Pakistan for so-called village rehab when their parents discover they are involved in criminal activities. Parents believe that the village offers a secure environment away from the allure of drugs – a chance to be socialized back into traditional *biradari* ways. However, as the following example of Shahid indicates, this seldom seems to work.

Shahid's uncle picks up the story of his nephew, as a cautionary tale which might prevent other young men from drifting into crime and drugs. Shahid was born in Britain, '[the] darling-of-the-house type person. Too much of a comfort zone they provided for him. I think because they did not keep pressure on him for education . . . that is why things went wrong.' Unknown to his family he was living a double life. 'Frustrated by the strict *biradari* regime . . . obligations and duties dictated by the elders, he rebelled. But it took them a while to realize that there was a problem. Shahid has started stealing to feed his drug habit. The final straw was when he got involved in a shooting incident. The family clubbed together for his ticket back to Pakistan for a dose of village rehab.'

The family preferred to send him to Pakistan rather than get him treated in Britain because that way his addiction could be hidden, since a visit to Pakistan was nothing out of the ordinary. Shahid's uncle points out that 'The reputation of the *biradari* must be protected at all costs. A scandal in one family will tarnish the honour of the whole clan.' What Shahid had done had damaged not only him, but his parents, brothers and sisters. By spiriting him off to Pakistan the family honour would not be compromised. Akhtar travels to Mirpur to find out whether such village rehab works, as well as to trace Shahid.

He visits a town in the heart of Pakistani-administered Kashmir.

> *The countryside is peppered with large villas owned by British Pakistani families. Building a large house back home in the ancestral village is a source of pride and a chance to show others how well you have done. But most are deserted . . . ghost villages whose inhabitants are thousands of miles away in Birmingham and Bradford.*[21] *[Still,] kids are sent here for a drugs free environment. But it is the*

exact opposite. The town has become a base for the drug barons of Afghanistan ... with one road in and out. It is a perfect place to co-ordinate their [drug] traffic operations. Ironically, the drugs here are being bought by the likes of Shahid in the UK.

Without money for medical treatment, village rehab seldom works. The problem is that the drugs from which parents hoped their sons would escape are cheaper locally and more readily available in purer form. Akhtar never did track down Shahid. He left, 'frustrated by the wall of silence that surrounds this problem. Once again, it seemed that the honour of the family and keeping up appearances was more important than seeking proper help'.

In Mirpur, Akhtar also attends a double wedding:

A traditional wedding band serenades the family. A brother and sister from America are marrying a girl from Birmingham and a boy from Mirpur, all from the same biradari *... [the] family from America and Britain have flown in to pay their respects ... if you do not turn up you suffer for years to come.* Biradari *weddings are lavish affairs. No expense has been spared. It is a case of keeping up with the Jats. In fact, the rivalries between* biradaris *over weddings got so out of hand that the [Pakistan] government recently introduced a law to restrict the size of celebrations.*

Tabassam from Bradford, a bridesmaid for the bride from Mirpur, answers Akhtar's question as to the meaning of *biradari* for her by saying: 'family relatives, your close first or second cousins ... and everyone who comes before and after you. That's *biradari*.' She tells him that she herself does not have a strong sense of *biradari*. She reluctantly goes along with a *biradari*-arranged marriage only after her parents veto her marriage with someone from outside it.

However, it is clear that a growing number of British Pakistanis are challenging tradition. British in education and socialization, they no longer feel committed to preserving the bloodline and upholding the honour of their clan. Sadly, this has become the source of family breakdowns. This is clear from a conversation Akhtar has with Zareena Khan, who hosts a weekly Mirpuri programme on the BBC's Asian Network – one of the few places where there is public debate about the *biradari*.

Khan rehearses cases where someone wants to marry a girl from a different *biradari* but the parents withhold their consent:

> *The girl is taken away to Pakistan so as to separate the couple . . . [or] I have seen some married off in Pakistan. When they return to this country they go back to their original relationship [although now married]. That does not help the community in a positive way. It causes misery whichever way you look at it.*

Akhtar talks to Asmat, who did the unthinkable by falling in love with a Jat outside her *biradari* whom she married against her parents' will. She was shocked that her educated father should press a *biradari* marriage upon her. She expresses bitterness at the fact that, rather than finding a suitable match based on compatibility of background, education and personality, the question was: 'Is he from our *biradari*? Then it does not matter whether he is blind or lame, you should marry him.'

Asmat is adamant that she will not let her children get embroiled in *biradari*-ism. Instead, like a growing number of British Pakistanis, she is appealing to Islam, with its insistence on a basic equality between all believers, to trump such parochial and restrictive loyalties.

The final issue which Akhtar raises in his programmes is the negative impact of *biradari*-ism on local politics in Britain. On the one hand, in Britain, men from modest artisan castes in Mirpur and low in the clan hierarchy have been able by sheer dint of ability to make their mark on local politics. One such was Muhammad Ajeeb, the first Asian Lord Mayor in Bradford in the mid-1980s. However, his rise was resented by those higher in the *biradari* hierarchy, such as the Rajputs and Jats. They responded by mobilizing *biradari* bloc votes to frustrate his selection as candidate for Parliament.

Akhtar makes clear that Mirpuri politicians also have an impact on British politics. He interviews an ex-prime minister of Pakistan-administered Kashmir, Sultan Mahmood Chaudhry. He proudly tells Akhtar that all four parliamentary seats in Kashmir belong to his Jat *biradari*. Indeed, an international Jat forum has been established with Sultan Mahmood and his father as patrons. He takes credit for being one of the first to recognize that in the UK the Jats could get elected to local government by mobilizing their *biradari* vote blocs.

Akhtar then speaks to Zafar Tanweer, a local Pakistani journalist based in Bradford who works for a Pakistani paper – *Daily Jang* – which produces a bilingual edition in Britain. Tanweer worries about the infiltration of such clan politics in Britain. He mentions his experience of a previous general election:

I saw that some people are supporting a candidate from one constituency and a second candidate from a different party in a different constituency ... not because they were the same party but both were Jat. Sultan Mahmood came here during the last election. He came to Bradford and supported one candidate standing for the Conservatives. In a second constituency in Sheffield he supported [a Jat] for a Liberal Democratic seat, and in a third supported a Jat standing for the Labour Party. They have no values, no respect [for the British system] and do not know or do not want to know about [British] party politics and policies.

Sultan Mahmood himself acknowledges 'helping' in 35 to 40 constituencies.

Next, Akhtar talks to Shahid Malik, a British-born Pakistani and member of Labour's National Executive Committee. Malik admits that the Labour Party has knowingly – or because of misplaced sensitivity to cultural norms – allowed *biradari* politics to flourish and that the British Pakistani and Kashmiri communities are held back by this clan mentality:

How and who people support has not been based on merit. And this has certainly had a major impact in letting down the British Pakistani community as a whole. The Labour Party – and other parties – got used to dealing with those people and there seems to be an unwitting collusion there between the political parties and the first generation Pakistanis ... Until the major parties take responsibility the clan mentality will continue. People will continue ... to abuse the democratic process.

Malik was cautiously optimistic that attitudes among the Labour hierarchy were changing with 'a realization that to continue to turn a blind eye is damaging democracy fundamentally and is not supporting inclusion, our big agenda ... [since] we are not seeing women and young people coming through the ranks.'

Such clan politics can exclude both able young people, male and female, within the *biradari* – since elders are preferred – and those who for reasons of principle oppose such politics. Either way, able young professionals who could represent the entire community, as well as articulate the concerns of their own community in an idiom which wider society understands, are frozen out. Where clan rather than competence dictates selection, young people within some of the most deprived wards are effectively disempowered. The presumption is that where patron–client politics of this sort is operative the beneficiaries will largely be fellow *biradari* members. To speak out against it takes courage since the individual faces social ostracism and even intimidation.

Akhtar concludes his radio programmes with the candid admission that

> *At present, there is a void between the first generation, who speaks for the community, and the second and third generations. This void continues to grow and is a cause of unrest with the young. My community needs to become more critical and demanding of its leadership. Open debate, the exchange of ideas and the promotion of merit, not clan loyalty, should be embraced. Forty years after arriving in Britain we are in danger of going backwards, divided by outdated and discriminatory practices.*

The new British: a gendered space

> I think a lot of young people are really screwed up [since] they do not make many decisions about their life.[22]

This opinion of an 18-year-old Bradford male sums up the somewhat bleak picture painted in recently published research of attitudes amongst a group of 14- to 19-year-olds from Mirpuri backgrounds. It is clear that family and *biradari* pressures fall disproportionately on young females.

Some 90 per cent describe themselves as British. By contrast, they consider 85 per cent of mothers and 70 per cent of fathers would describe themselves as Pakistani. Eight out of ten prefer English music to 'Asian' music, while one in six enjoy both; similar preferences are expressed with regard to films. Seven out of ten girls enjoy the same magazines as their English peers but, in addition, buy those which feature Bollywood stars.

Most of these young people find it difficult to relate to parents and elders. This is rooted in different lifestyles, attitudes and experiences. Less than one in ten feel the elders understand their feelings and needs. This is tantamount to a communication crisis across the generations. Most young people know that sensitive issues, such as marriage, are simply taboo. The person in whom they can confide tends to be a cousin. They are also weary of sectarian differences in the community, which means that many are dissuaded from socializing with members of other Islamic sects. They blame parents and religious leaders for importing such differences into Britain. They believe that differences between *biradaris* based on sect and caste are as pronounced as differences between Pakistanis and Indians, or whites and Asians.

More than eight out of ten males and females would prefer to select their own marriage partner. As well as wanting choice, they are anxious about the incompatibility of spouses from Pakistan. They are aware that for their parents such partners are preferred because they are thought to reinforce traditional values and gender hierarchy and cement *biradari* connections.

English films, music and magazines are frowned upon by many parents, some of whom even search their daughters' bedrooms for offending materials. For the young, this smacks of hypocrisy, since many parents listen to Asian music and films – valued as a vehicle for preserving their own culture. Indeed, to walk around an 'Asian' neighbourhood is to trip over video shops renting out such films. The sentiments and actions of such films are just as trangressive of strict Islamic norms as those of many English films!

In all, such restrictions have generated a female subculture largely hidden from parental and *biradari* scrutiny. This is usually played out in school or when the girls go truant: a third of girls and boys admitted to going truant. Their topics of discussion turn on issues of freedom, from the right to choose a dress code to the right to wear make-up. 'They felt restricted in their choice of hairstyle; restricted in their ability to freely listen to English music or watch English films; forbidden to participate in sports after school and forbidden from socializing with friends outside school, even from going to town or to the cinema.'[23]

What is clear from their interviews is that many have lost respect for parental and *biradari* norms. Time and again, as young people are wont to do, they see evidence of hypocrisy. They seem to spend a lot of their energy developing strategies to circumvent such restrictions, perceived to be unfair. Young women rail against double standards with regard to gender. A 16-year-old girl complained bitterly that

> *My father doesn't want us to go out at night with friends. He doesn't want us to have freedom. But boys can go out anywhere they want, many of them have cars, they hang about in gangs with white girls. Nobody says anything to them simply because they're boys.*[24]

Unsurprisingly, young men often internalize, as well as challenge, such distinct gender roles. Studies in London and the north of England make clear that young men take advantage of the relative laxity of parents to engage in irreligious behaviour. At the same time, they establish their Muslim credentials by insisting on 'the virtuous conduct of their wives, sisters and daughters'.[25]

Like many other adolescents from a working-class background, the young men of Pakistani and Bangladeshi heritage express the usual marks of 'laddishness' at school, whether hanging out with mates, being good at sport, having the right sort of clothes or not being seen to work too hard. However, in addition, some assert their masculinity by presuming to police their sisters' behaviour and dress codes – justified by an appeal to protecting honour, culture and tradition.

In conversation with each other, they are likely to boast about the retribution they will visit on an erring sister seen going out with a boy. At the same time, it is fine for them to go out with white girls. Such gendered double standards are justified by recourse to the notion of 'reputation': 'The argument being that girls' behaviours reflect upon the family reputations, whereas boys' do not. Thus the boys claimed that by going out with white girls, they were actually respecting the reputation of Muslim girls and their families'![26] While the young men posture amongst themselves about defending their sisters' honour, in reality this is little more than fiction and fantasy. Their sisters, after all, are outperforming them at school and are better equipped for higher education.

However, when the girls get to college or university, supervision and double standards often continue. This is the conclusion of a female Islamic Studies lecturer, Haiffa Jawad – herself a Muslim, from Iraq – in a monograph on Muslim women in the UK. She bases her comments on nine years of lecturing British Muslim students in Birmingham, many of whom have been young women from South Asian backgrounds. She observes that within many South Asian families, women are discouraged from continuing in education; if they stand up for their rights they are accused of bringing 'shame' to the family. Indeed, 'female education is viewed as a threat to the traditional customs and way of life of the community'. She speaks of a personal encounter with the husband of one of her students, who complained that 'I was causing his family to break up, saying: "... you are teaching our women their rights and encouraging them to rebel against the status quo"'. Dr Jawad is not intimidated by such accusations. As the author of a work on women's rights in Islam, she insists that the husband's perspective is at odds with Muhammad's views on female education.[27]

It's good to talk: the Muslim Youth Helpline

Clearly, for many young Muslims, not least those with parents having roots in rural societies, growing up in Britain can be a testing experience – especially since 9/11 and 7/7, when their communities have been exposed to unprecedented media scrutiny. The absence of support networks for young people within the Muslim communities, and an anxious feeling that mainstream provision is unaware of their particular conflicts rooted in multiple identities, leaves many youngsters isolated: 'For many Muslims, the feeling of never quite belonging and having to meet conflicting social expectations, creates despair during the formative years of adulthood.'[28]

To meet this need, the Muslim Youth Helpline (MYH) was established, providing a unique service for young people by young people. It makes no grandiose claims to represent this or that community, but rather aims to reflect and address the concerns of young Muslims themselves. It provides a safe space for the discussion of problems which young people traditionally have to suffer in silence because of the fear of family reprisal and the stigma attached: depression, (homo) sexuality, drugs, family tensions and relationships. Too often the fear of bringing dishonour on their families exacerbates their isolation.

MYH was started by a group of young Muslim college students (aged 16–19) in 2001. It has gone from strength to strength. October 2004 saw the launch of <www.muslimyouth.net> – an online forum to discuss social and mental health concerns, serviced by volunteers, young writers and photographers, who produce and maintain the site. The emphasis is on peer support: its volunteers are 16 to 25 years old, as are most of its management team and board of trustees. Although based in London, more than half its users are from other locations across the country. MYH's professed aim is to provide a confidential and non-judgemental support, guidance and counselling service which is faith- and culture-sensitive. Apart from six full-time staff, the majority of its 45 helpline workers and supervisors are volunteers.

This somewhat dry analysis belies the content of their websites and the range of its outreach, mentoring and counselling services. Controversial and sensitive issues are addressed in a youth-friendly language. Their website is marked by candour, robust debate and humour. 'Blog of the month' – an online diary – is an abstract from a longer piece entitled 'Ningas on the Loose', from a gently self-parodying group of Muslim women. Alongside this is much sensible advice, whether in response to e-mails from a young man worried that he will go to hell if he continues to masturbate, or to a moving e-mail from a young man in prison for whom MYH was literally a lifeline.

The spread of materials – articles, chat rooms, campaigns, surveys, competitions – are invariably insightful and amusing, encompassing articles on how to cope with pushy parents, Muslim rapping, *halal* socializing, tuition fees for college, and arranged marriage. Also, contemporary political issues are discussed in a no-holds-barred chat room – the pros and cons of an Islamic state, making sense of 7/7, and how to dispel fear of Islam in a media context where Islam has been equated with terror. A young Londoner shocked by 7/7 urged his fellow-believers to involve themselves in shared vigils and to give blood to show their solidarity with a grieving city.

Such catchy items as 'Chick of the Month' and 'Stud of the Month' feature role models for the young, such as Hannah Al-Rashid, a young woman who has recently won a European martial arts title, or the successful boxer Amir Khan. Discussion sites are full of robustly argued material by feisty females on gender relations and equality in marriage. Such material offers a reformist reading of Qur'anic texts, providing a more congenial alternative to the traditionalist guidance offered to women in the *Heavenly Ornaments* genre.

One of its campaigns urged the young to participate in civic life. Since some 60,000 Muslims in London have not yet registered to vote, a provocative article urged them to register for the 2007 elections so as to keep the British National Party out, not least because the BNP 'badmouth Islam to get votes'.

MYH is conscious of the centrality of music in young people's lives. Its Youth Voices project has provided an opportunity for young Muslims to express their social concerns through music: 'Eight talented young Muslim artists were chosen to work on producing a musical CD, each track highlighting a different social concern that young Muslims could face in modern Britain. The project culminated in a musical performance evening, where songs from the CD were performed live on stage'.[29] This is but one of a number of imaginative outreach programmes MYH now run.

MYH is an excellent example of that 'open debate, the exchange of ideas and the promotion of merit' for which Navid Akhtar argued as a counter to the debilitating impact of clan norms. Much of its content supports its director Shareefa Fulat's contention that the acquisition of a robust Muslim identity can enhance the confidence of young Muslims and encourage them to participate in civic life. For women, there are interpretations of Islam which are genuinely emancipatory, enabling them to 'combat traditional taboos of communities ... often mistaken as Islamic oppression. For example, there is no basis in Islam for forced marriages, or so-called honour killings, and the appropriate knowledge of the teachings of Islam are a powerful tool in challenging community attitudes that tolerate such practices'.[30]

Notes

1. S. Fulat, 'Caught between Two Worlds: How Can the State Help Young Muslims?', in M. Bunting (ed.), *Islam, Race and Being British* (London: *Guardian* in association with Barrow Cadbury Trust, 2005), p. 69.

2. *Telegraph and Argus*, 29 June 2003.

3. M. Y. Alam, *Kilo* (Glasshoughton: Route, 2002), p. 43.

4. Ibid., pp. 150–1.

5. Ibid., p. 116.

6. Ibid., p. 204.

7. M. Quraishi, *Muslims and Crime: A Comparative Study* (Aldershot: Ashgate, 2005), p. 99.

8. Quotations from, and paraphrases of, this talk are based on the transcript I made when it was delivered.

9. See B. Metcalf, *Perfecting Women: Maulana Ashraf 'Ali Thanawis' Bihishti Zewar* (Heavenly Ornaments) (London: University of California Press, 1990).

10. A. Katz, *Thwarted Dreams: Young Views from Bradford* (East Molesey, Surrey: Young Voice, 2002), p. 9.

11. Ibid., p. 33.

12. R. Richardson and A. Wood, *The Achievement of British Pakistani Learners: Work in Progress* (Stoke-on-Trent: Trentham Books, 2004), p. 51.

13. R. Razwan, *Fathers' Involvement in their Children's Upbringing and Education* (London: Children's Society, 2002), p. 30.

14. Ibid., p. 7.

15. A. Jalal, *The State of Martial Rule: The Origins of Pakistan's Political Economy of Defence* (Cambridge: Cambridge University Press, 1990), p. 292.

16. I. Din, *The New British: The Impact of Culture and Community on Young Pakistanis* (Aldershot: Ashgate, 2006), p. 98.

17. A. Sahin, 'Exploring the Religious Life-World and Attitudes toward Islam among British Muslim Adolescents', in L. J. Francis, M. Robbins and J. Astley, *Religion, Education and Adolescence: International Empirical Perspectives* (Cardiff: University of Wales, 2005), p. 179.

18. Metcalf, *Perfecting Women*, p. 23.

19. V. Kalra, *From Textile Mills to Taxi Ranks: Experiences of Migration, Labour and Social Change* (Aldershot: Ashgate, 2000), pp. 156–7.

20. These programmes, both titled 'The Biradari', were originally broadcast on 26 August and 2 September 2003. Quotations and paraphrases are based on

my own transcripts. For those curious to know more about the history and dynamics of caste and tribe in Pakistan, see Pierre Lafranc, 'Between Caste and Tribe', in C. Jaffrelot (ed.), *A History of Pakistan and its Origins* (London: Anthem Press, 2004).

21. This echoes an anthropologist's 'dominant image' of 'a tour of Mirpuri villages ... [with] padlocks on large gates on even larger households': Kalra, *From Textile Mills to Taxi Ranks*, p. 70.

22. Quoted in Din, *The New British*, p. 144.

23. Ibid., p. 126.

24. Ibid., p. 128.

25. J. Jacobsen, *Islam in Transition: Religion and Identity among British Pakistani Youth* (London: Routledge, 1998), p. 121.

26. L. Archer, *Race, Masculinity and Schooling: Muslim Boys and Education* (Maidenhead: Open University Press, 2003), p. 82.

27. H. Jawad, 'Historical and Contemporary Perspectives of Muslim Women Living in the West', in T. Benn and H. A. Jawad (eds), *Muslim Women in the United Kingdom and Beyond: Experiences and Images* (Leiden: Brill, 2004), pp. 2–3.

28. S. Fuat and R. Jaffrey, 'Muslim Youth Helpline: A Model of Youth Engagement in Service Delivery', *Youth and Policy*, 92 (Summer 2006), p. 152.

29. Ibid., p. 166.

30. Fulat, 'Caught between Two Worlds', p. 70.

CHAPTER 3

Debating Islam: Muslim Professionals Find their Voice

After graduating from University College, London in the late 1990s, Asim Siddiqui went to work in the City. As a Muslim activist on campus, he and a few friends had wanted to create a space in London where professionals could meet and socialize – a '*halal* alternative' to the Friday night pub culture – and discuss the many issues exercising young British Muslims. They had also wanted to provide practical opportunities to put something back into their communities. Asim was aware that the absence of such a space meant the Muslim communities were losing some of their brightest and best, especially female graduates.

When it came to defining such a space, a critical moment for Asim had been the presence on campus of two Muslim groups producing literature defining what was to count as an Islamic state. Both drew on Islam's authoritative textual sources, yet came to radically incompatible conclusions! Yet there was no dialogue between such groups, compounding the confusion of impressionable Muslim students. As a result, after leaving university Asim and a group of friends created the City Circle in 1999.[1]

The main aim of this chapter is to profile a range of such initiatives across the UK – where young professionals are beginning to develop a distinctive British Muslim perspective on a range of pressing practical and theoretical issues. The intention is to capture something of the creativity and idealism energizing such developments. Often, they take place outside formal Muslim organizations – still largely dominated by elders born outside Britain. Sometimes they take place within them, with British Muslims seeking to nudge the old guard to a more open engagement with other Muslim traditions and the wider society. Others are issue-based and independent. However, like the Muslim Youth Helpline, discussed in the previous chapter, they do not close the door on continuing dialogue with Islamic religious scholars.

The City Circle: thinking outside the box

From the beginning the ethos of the City Circle was to provide an independent, safe and open space for its weekly Friday evening debates: independent of any one Muslim tradition, group or organization, domestic or foreign; a safe space with ground rules to enable honest and critical debate on controversial issues; open to all who would respect its ground rules. Unlike many Muslim organizations, there is no separate women's section. No dress code is specified as a condition for admission. In August 2000, the Circle packed the LSE's old lecture theatre to discuss global warming with George Monbiot, the veteran environmental campaigner, as the invited expert. As Asim remarks, in a piece written for a Fabian Society conference, 'learning from non-Muslim scholars was innovative for its time'.[2]

After 9/11, from within the City Circle ranks, an anti-war group emerged which formed a part of the 'Stop the War' coalition, urging Muslims to march alongside their compatriots. Such collaboration with non-Muslims generated some resentment and confusion, given the wider context in which Muslim groups traditionally projected Islamic authenticity in terms of difference from the non-Muslim. To address such anxieties the City Circle organized a conference in November 2001 on 'Islam and the Peace Movement – Where Do We Stand?', inviting Muslim scholars to justify the position they were taking.

All in all, the City Circle is encouraging Muslims to be 'more open-minded, self-critical and less holier-than-thou'.[3] Speakers are encouraged to say openly and honestly what they would be reluctant to say in front of their own immediate Islamic circle or tradition. Such a process generated an address in April 2004 on 'The Muslim Obsession with Themselves' delivered by a Wahhabi/Salafi scholar – a Saudi-based tradition not known for its self-criticism. As Asim notes in his contribution for the Fabian Society, 'such criticism of "religious Muslims" would previously have been considered treason'. The City Circle's approach is not to seek to impose solutions but rather 'to ask the right questions'.

Asim recalls that while many of the men are content with debating theological minutiae, it is the women who are heading up the community projects and find themselves setting the agenda. Their social, welfare and educational projects depend both on people giving their time voluntarily and also convincing their companies to release them to contribute to such philanthropic activities. In this they seem to have been very successful. The City Circle website has a comprehensive listing of activities which range from career workshops and mentoring programmes at Tower Hamlets College, a Saturday school with activities for 160 students aged 8 to 18, a homeless project responding to need, irrespective of background or religion, to a Montessori *madrasa*. This last was set up in 2003, with the aim of providing children with 'an integrated and inter-active approach to the study of the Qur'an and the Arabic language – a counter to the rote learning offered by traditional madrasa'.[4]

What is surprising is that the City Circle does not use the terms 'Islamic' or 'Muslim' to describe itself. This reflects a number of factors. First, they are impatient with the view that Muslims need to rally under a separate Muslim banner on all issues. Indeed, those in the network are urged, where possible, to join mainstream groups with fellow-citizens. So, if they are concerned with foreign policy they should join groups such as Amnesty International; if they have an issue with civil liberties they should join pressure groups such as Liberty. Secondly, the Circle's emphasis is on promoting universal values considered part of but not exclusive to the Islamic tradition and shared by most citizens. This enables them to offer the wider community an open space in which to have a two-way dialogue around shared social problems.

Further, for the professionals who attend City Circle events, 'innovation' is second nature. They relish the challenge of being at the heart of a global city. While City Circle is non-sectarian, its stance towards Islam might be characterized as respectful of tradition but impatient of traditionalism. To cite a well-known epigram, where 'tradition is the living faith of the dead, traditionalism is the dead faith of the living'.[5] This is clear in a statement of the Circle's values:

> *If sectarian interpretations of Islam get in the way of Muslim unity then ideologically-obsessed interpretations of Islam get in the way of bringing Muslim and non-Muslim communities together. We should not be importing religious or political ideologies from the Middle East or Pakistan but instead be developing a distinct compassionate British Islam – or a European Islam as our speaker Tariq Ramadan would*

> *say – and exporting that to the Muslim world. The Muslim world needs as much help as we can give them and importing their conflicts into the UK does not help them nor does it help us.*[6]

This statement of values adds that 'we do our soul searching in public'. This is no exaggeration. To download their weekly talks is to enter a world of robust, frequently exhilarating argumentation, at turns passionate and poignant. Immediately after 7/7 the City Circle assembled speakers to discuss the theme of 'The Criminal Distortion of Islamic Texts'. 7/7 underlined the importance for Muslims to come out of their 'mental and physical ghettos and to join the mainstream'.

The event was written up in the *Guardian* by Madeleine Bunting, a journalist who has an exemplary record of enabling the voices of young British Muslims to be heard in her column.[7] This article has been reproduced on the City Circle website and includes her comment about one of the speakers, a Salafi imam, Abu Muntasir. To the question how Qur'anic verses about jihad had been used to legitimize 7/7, he 'patiently tried to answer – it's been a failure of our scholars, a failure of our teachers. The harshness of the self-criticism was painful to hear: this was a community flagellating itself'.

However, the weekly talks are far more than self-laceration. The speakers are drawn from the growing pool of distinguished Muslim writers, academics and religious scholars within Britain, as well as from across the Muslim world. A British academic, Iftikhar Malik, argues for the need to retrieve 'Muslim Civil Society – The Lost Heritage of Islam'. An Egyptian scholar, Hassan Hanafi, clarifies what an Islamic civil society today might look like. An evening is devoted to a conversation with the reformist thinker Anwar Ibrahim, a former deputy prime minister of Malaysia. The Indian scholar Dr Asghar Ali Engineer deconstructs the notion of an Islamic state, insisting that whatever state approximates to the key Qur'anic values of justice, benevolence, compassion and wisdom would qualify as an Islamic state, irrespective of the label attached to it.

This message is driven home in a sharp contribution by one of the few public intellectuals amongst British Muslims, Ziauddin Sardar, who writes for the *New Statesman*. Sardar reminds his audience that the contemporary Muslim 'obsession' with political power obscures the reality that real power turns on a knowledge-rich society. Many Muslim majority societies have yet to learn this lesson; too often those with oil wealth assume they can simply buy knowledge. He refers to a UN publication in 2003 compiled by a distinguished group of Arab thinkers – the *Arab Human Development Report* – to indicate the woeful state of translation of works into Arabic: 'The aggregate total of translated books from the Al-Ma'mun era [d. 813] to the present day amounts to 10,000 books – equivalent to what Spain translates [into Spanish] in a single year.'[8]

Sardar, in part, blames the dead hand of traditionalism, which is content to imitate previous scholars rather than examine and build on their work. This generates a religious culture which denies personal agency to the individual; the Muslim becomes an empty vessel into which the *'ulama* pour knowledge. These ideas are developed in his engaging autobiography, *Desperately Seeking Paradise: Journeys of a Sceptical Muslim*, one of a number of works the City Circle has profiled and discussed. *Desperately Seeking Paradise* is a *tour d'horizon* of the intellectual and spiritual condition of the contemporary Muslim world, informed by a rare blend of wit and insight, enlivened by wonderfully indiscreet pen portraits of leading personalities.

The City Circle weekly meetings also provide a platform for spiritual reflection, entertainment and artistic performance, from the serious to the light-hearted. One recent presentation, given by an American, Dr Umar F. Abd-Allah, is provocatively entitled 'Cultural jihad'. He asks:

> *What needs to be done to convert Western society to associate Islam with the beauty of the Taj Mahal and the majesty of the Dome of the Rock rather than with the blasted Twin Towers of New York or the shattered Buddhist statues in Afghanistan? Can we develop an agenda of cultural do's that would harness the energy of our young people; to teach them that singing, creating, beautifying and being joyous are all part of the Islamic agenda?*[9]

Luqman Ali is a frequent visitor to the Circle. His most recent address was entitled 'Self-knowledge – Resource for Reconciliation'. Ali is co-founder of Khayaal, a professional theatre company offering experience of Muslim world culture through contemporary art forms. Another evening had the intriguing title 'Allah Made Him Funny' – the American Muslim stand-up comedian, Azhar Usman, held the floor.

Along with providing a platform for some of the most stimulating thinkers, the City Circle has gained a reputation for promoting the discussion of contentious intra- and inter-community topics which hit the headlines. One example will suffice. This was a conversation between Martin Bright, the political editor of the *New Statesman*, Madeleine Bunting of the *Guardian*, Iqbal Sacranie, an ex-Director-General of the Muslim Council of Britain (MCB), and Yahya Birt, an academic who advises City Circle. The topic was 'Who Should Government Talk To?' This was a response to a controversial Channel 4 programme and a pamphlet written by Bright.

In this pamphlet, Bright, drawing on leaked Foreign Office (FCO) documents, demonstrated that the mandarins dealing with the Middle East felt they had no choice but to engage in dialogue with the Islamists – especially the Muslim Brotherhood – since their star seemed, at present, in the ascendancy. However, these same officials were also dealing with British Muslim issues. It was this crossover between the national and international which concerned Bright. He cited advice given by an Islamic issues adviser within the FCO not to ban named Islamists from coming into Britain. One was a Bangladeshi politician, Delwar Hossain Sayeedi, with a particularly unsavoury past; another, the controversial Qatar-based scholar Shaikh Yusuf al-Qaradawi. Both were tendentiously depicted as part of the Muslim 'mainstream', whether in Bangladesh or the Arab world.

Bright represented the MCB, established in 1997, as little more than an Islamist creature of two former Home Secretaries, one a Conservative, Michael Howard, the other Labour, Jack Straw. By allowing it to become the main interlocutor with government, Bright contended, the majority of Muslims, who did not adhere to the Islamist tradition, had been crowded out. Indeed, this dissatisfaction with MCB had expressed itself in the creation of two new bodies, the British Muslim Forum (BMF) and the Sufi Muslim Council, which sought to organize and articulate what they claimed was the silent voice of the majority – especially within the South Asian communities.

Bright's pamphlet includes an introduction by Jason Burke, a specialist on radical Islam, who commended it as a valuable contribution which dealt head on with a number of critical questions, namely:

> *How do we engage with radical Islam? Can we separate the violent radicals who want to destroy and replace the modern state from the political Islamists who want to appropriate it? . . . Whose voices best represent the complex, diverse and dynamic societies that are bundled*

> *together in that terrible generalisation, the 'Muslim world'? ... neither bin Laden and his jihadis, nor political Islamists like those of the Muslim Brotherhood, have a monopoly on the representation of the views and aspirations of the world's Muslims.*[10]

A lively debate ensued which illuminated some of the vexed issues concerning the representation of Britain's hugely diverse Muslim communities. First, it was plausibly argued, *contra* Bright, that the government had realized that it could not simply turn to one organization to capture this diversity.[11] Secondly, Bright had made the mistake of blaming Islamism *tout simple* for terrorism. This ignores the huge diversity within the phenomena labelled Islamism or 'political Islam' across the Muslim world, which encompasses reformists, radicals and extremists. To name a movement 'Islamist' is to leave open whether or not it embraces violence as a political strategy: some do, others do not.

A contribution to the City Circle by the Egyptian-born Swiss academic and activist Tariq Ramadan – grandson of the founder of the Muslim Brotherhood – helpfully clarified the nature of violent Islamism as a combination of three factors: a Manichaean mind-set which thinks in terms of 'us versus them'; a preoccupation with the capture of political power; and a willingness to use violence to achieve their goals.

Thirdly, any attempt to organize Muslims in Britain, especially those with roots in South Asia, is always going to be hostage to an entrenched sectarian division within the Sunni tradition imported from those countries. Because one of these schools of thought – Deobandis – has aligned itself with the MCB, only a few people in the other – Barelwis – feel comfortable in the same organization. Indeed, both the British Muslim Forum and the Sufi Muslim Council are largely home to this latter tradition. Therefore, representation is always going to be a work in progress. So long as institution-building continues to be dominated by those born elsewhere, sectarian disputes within those countries will be kept alive in Britain.

Fourthly, Bright's interpretation of Islam perpetuates another unhelpful binary opposition: Sufi good, Islamist bad! Bright assumes that Sufis are apolitical and simply concerned with cultivating the inner life. This is a decidedly partial understanding of Sufism. As pointed out at the meeting, they often led military movements against colonialism in the nineteenth century. Furthermore, political Islam emerged in

Egypt and India in the 1920s and 1930s among urban professionals, in part, as a protest against an institutionalized Sufism, inextricably interwoven with a compromised rural elite. That protest was not without foundation – namely, that, 'exploited by shaykhs whose influence over them was complete, victimized Muslims "resigned" themselves to their economic and social "fate"'.[12] This was anathema to the activist mentality of the Islamists concerned with 'social justice'. As a political editor of a left-wing weekly, one might have expected Bright to register some understanding of this dimension of Islamism, whatever criticisms one can legitimately make of other aspects of their ideology.

The City Circle remains one of the few places where non-Muslims can overhear some of these passionate debates exercising young British Muslims. Their speakers also include rabbis and activists involved in the growing interfaith movement. It says much for the reputation they now command in political and media circles that Jack Straw MP was prepared to explain and debate the position he took on the *niqab* – the face-veil – at one of their weekly meetings.

The City Circle is convinced that there is a growing constituency across the country for this sort of network. To this end, they have recently appointed a director to establish counterparts, initially in Birmingham and Manchester, and to extend the range of their volunteer-led projects at the grassroots. By multiplying such spaces for open debate, the hope is to clarify a vision and direction for the future of Britain's Muslim communities.

Q-News: nursery for Muslim journalism

In a poignant work entitled *Will We Have Jewish Grandchildren?* Sir Jonathan Sacks, the present Chief Rabbi, has written frankly about the challenges facing Jews in Western societies:

> *We know the rules governing relationships between Jew and Jew, but our understanding of the relationships between Jew and non-Jew in a plural and interdependent world is far from clear ... We know that going to synagogue or keeping* kashrut *is Jewish. Yet, we are not sure that there is a Judaic way of being an academic or a journalist or an artist or an architect or a politician. When Jews speak in the public arena, they often confuse Jewish self-interests ... with Judaic principle.*[13]

Young British Muslims trained in a variety of professions are struggling with these same questions. The focus here will be on what is to count as a Muslim journalist. Next we will consider the world of the Muslim youth worker and teacher. These three professions have been chosen because they have the potential to shape and guide a new generation.

When a definitive history of British Muslims comes to be written, Fuad Nahdi will be seen to have been one of its most formative and creative influences. As a distinguished journalist himself, he founded *Q-News* in 1992. It was intended both as a Muslim community publication and as a vehicle to encourage young people into the profession. It has been successful on both fronts. Nationally, the quality of its journalism makes it the first point of entry for understanding the concerns and anxieties exercising the Muslim communities.

A Muslim journalist who writes for the mainstream media will often have developed their skills at *Q-News*. Three young journalists immediately come to mind: Faisal Bodi, who contributes to such broadsheets as the *Independent* and the *Guardian*; Ehsan Masood, who writes for the political monthly *Prospect*; and Fareena Alam, *Q-News*'s current editor, who frequently appears in print and electronic media. In an address to the Foreign Press Association in 2003, Fuad admitted that

> *From the beginning we had to provide answers to many fundamental questions: What* is *a Muslim publication? How would it essentially differ from other publications? To what extent should it be a campaigning tool, as opposed to a reporting organ?*
>
> *I am afraid . . . we still don't have all the clear answers. But we know that without credibility – without the fact that we are just and fair and seen to be just and fair, there is no future for any media outlet.*[14]

In the same address, he worried that the draconian anti-terrorist legislation, coupled with the mainstream media's general neglect of serious and informed commentary on Muslim communities, 'guarantees the burgeoning presence of an underground media which runs completely parallel to the mainstream, never engaging. The course of the continuing Muslim diatribe against "the West" now raging particularly on the internet will depend on how strong Muslim journalists and media in the West are.'

Leafing through its back numbers, various themes and emphases relevant to this book become apparent. First, as with its present editor, the voice of Muslim women is increasingly heard. More than a decade ago, a Muslim women's helpline in Wembley congratulated *Q-News* for opening up the issue of abuse of women in the Muslim community, as well as pointing out that they were 'inundated' with calls from young women being prevented from pursuing higher education or 'married women ... more or less imprisoned within four walls ... [who] end up on tranquillizers, anti-depressants or Prozac'.[15]

Humera Khan, founder member of a Muslim woman's organization, An-Nisa, noted that since 'most Muslim organizations are void of women and young people', women have busied themselves with 'getting training in education, media, social work, health care and counselling. Muslim women are now a quiet but potent presence in statutory bodies and other public arenas increasingly becoming team managers, directors of departments and chairs of committees. Women's organizations have led the way in setting agendas and developing much needed social welfare projects that support families and heal communities.'[16]

Secondly, seeking to preserve its independence, *Q-News* denounced the importation of sectarian rabble-rousers from South Asia, who routinely visit Britain on preaching tours. In the mid-1990s an editorial thundered against an invitation which had been extended to one Zia ur Rahman, leader of the 'odious Sipah-e Sahaba', a rabidly anti-Shia, Deobandi extremist group, involved in tit-for-tat sectarian killings of Shias in Pakistan.

It is clear from letters and questions to their resident Islamic law expert, who wrote an agony uncle column in the 1990s – an Egyptian scholar, the late Sheikh Darsh – that British Muslims have been increasingly exasperated by the importation of sectarianism from back home. For example, Dr Darsh sympathized with a Deobandi questioner perplexed by constantly being told not to worship in Barelwi mosques because they prefix the vocative 'Ya' to the name of the Prophet. Sheikh Darsh explained that

> *One school of thought approves of the prefix which they say indicates that the Prophet is capable of seeing, hearing and generally interceding for suppliants. Others believe supplication should be directed to God alone because he alone has these attributes ... However, today many young people are being brainwashed into regarding this as an act of* shirk *['associating' the created with the Creator, i.e. idolatry] – a reaction which is causing lots of dissension and hostility amongst our community.*[17]

In the late 1990s and early years of this century the criticisms intensify, as it becomes clear that extremist ideologies have found a home amongst a section of young British Muslims. In 1999 *Q-News* profiled Abu Hamza al-Masri, a self-styled 'shaikh' who had taken over the Finsbury Park mosque. Hamza, an Egyptian with an engineering degree from Britain, had lost an eye and both hands in Afghanistan in 1993. In 1994 he set up the Supporters of Shariah (SoS) with other veterans of the Afghan war.

In 1999 five Britons, including Hamza's son, his son-in-law, and the press officer of SoS, were found guilty in Yemen of planning a number of attacks in Aden – whose targets included a church, a hotel and the British consulate. All were given sentences of between three and seven years. The British government's position was that they had not received a fair trial. But Hamza himself, who was not among the defendants arrested in Yemen, was subsequently arrested in London and found guilty of soliciting murder and incitement to racial hatred, the latter because of his vitriolic anti-Jewish comments. He was sentenced to seven years in prison in 2006 and is awaiting extradition proceedings to stand trial in the USA.

In an extended interview with Hamza in 1999, the *Q-News* journalist, Shagufta Yaqub, is clearly appalled by his answers to her questions. She asks pointedly: 'So Muslims should go to fight, blow up a few limbs and then come back to Britain, like yourself?' To which he answers: 'This is what the *Sahaba* [the Prophet's companions] have done. I am telling you about the religion ... of the messenger of God. If the *Sahaba* had gone to work with the Romans and clean their toilets like Muslims are doing here, then you would never have been a Muslim now. The *Sahaba* have taken the initiative, they took the sword, they gave the message'.

To her question, 'Do you feel any responsibility for contributing to the Western media stereotype of Muslims as terrorists and religious fanatics? ... How good can that be for inviting non-Muslims to Islam?', he answers defiantly: 'It is because you are defeated inside that you think this is true. Have you ever seen non-Muslims queuing to come to Islam ... Instead we have seen Muslims queuing to go out of Islam by being lesbian and gay and using interest-based mortgages. If you cannot keep your Islamic identity why are you thinking about one John or Shirley who comes to Islam every blue moon, and doesn't last long anyway'. To her final question – 'This whole [Yemeni] episode has come at a time when a section of the British Muslim community are quite happy with their acceptance into British society. They believe that finally some doors have been opened for them in the corridors of power. What advice would you give to these people?' – he replies, 'Islam says to be a tail in the truth is better than to be a head in falsehood'.[18]

Fuad Nahdi, in the same issue, reflects that 'in the run-down alleys and high streets of Britain we have a production line whereby Abu Hamzas are run off by the minute'. The fact that such a demagogue without 'deep spirituality or sagacity' can attract substantial numbers of decent young people provides a window into the 'psychological and spiritual condition' of some Muslim communities. A number of factors are identified which cumulatively begin to explain such a phenomenon: social exclusion, racism, Islamophobia, 'irrelevant religious teachings which lack both soul or intellectual content'. Nahdi quotes a mother of a teenager who is a member of SoS: 'What is better: that my son dies a drug addict or a mujahid fighting for Islam?' However 'far-fetched and surreal' such a proposition sounds, Nahdi concludes, this is 'exactly [the] kind of mindset that motivates and inspires [them]'.[19]

Inevitably, 9/11 led to a great deal of soul-searching within the pages of the magazine. One of the most impressive contributions was written by Hamza Yusuf, the influential American Sufi shaikh cited in an earlier chapter. In a piece entitled 'A Time for Introspection', he bewails the presence of two sorts of related extremism within the community. The first is those 'reactionary extremists [who] do not want any pluralism; they view the world in melodramatic, black and white [terms] ... They are good and anyone who opposes them is evil ... they use *takfir* [excommunication] and character assassination as a tool for marginalising any criticism'. The second is 'radical extremists ... [who] differ [from the first group] in that they will use violence to further their cause'.[20] Hamza Yusuf dubs the latter group *kharijites* – seceders – the prototypical violent zealots of Islamic history. They emerged soon after the Prophet's death in 632 when the nascent Muslim community was wracked by civil war. Although defeated, their Manichaean world-view, which divided all Muslims into one of two camps – the 'People of Heaven' and the 'People of Hell' – was 'adopted by succeeding generations of extremists to give religious sanction to their political rebellions against both Muslim and non-Muslim governments'.[21]

In seeking to explain the salience of such groups today, Hamza Yusuf is unsparing in his criticism of the *'ulama* and the hollowing-out of the Islamic tradition:

> *Islam has been hijacked by a discourse of anger and the rhetoric of rage [broadcast from pulpits] in which people with often recognisable psychopathology use anger . . . to rile Muslims up, only to leave them bitter and spiteful towards [non-Muslim] people who in the most part are completely unaware of the conditions in the Muslim world, or of the oppressive assaults of some Western countries on Muslim peoples. We have lost our bearings because we have lost our theology. We have almost no theologians in the entire Muslim world . . . [Muslims] generally prefer to attack the West as the sole reason for their problems when the truth is we are bankrupt as a religious community . . . Where is our media? Where . . . our spokespeople? Where our scholars? Where our literary figures? The truth is we don't have any – and so instead of looking inward and asking painful questions . . . we take the simple way out by attacking people.*[22]

A related theme which *Q-News* explores is the increasing expression of Muslim radicalism on the university campus. A detailed piece by Yahya Birt entitled 'Fear and Loathing on Campus', written in 2002, provides an insightful overview of the changing face of Muslim campus politics.[23] Birt argues that the Federation of Student Islamic Societies (FOSIS), from its heyday in the 1980s as a carrier of 'the patient politics of negotiation and engagement', has been effectively dead in London, the heartland of Muslim student activity, since the late 1990s.

The 'foremost factor' in the present disarray, he argues, was the rise of Hizb ut-Tahrir (HT) in the 1980s and then of a breakaway group from HT, al Muhajirun, in 1996, 'which coarsened and radicalised political debate among Muslim students'. Hizb ut-Tahrir, founded in Palestine in the 1950s, had itself split from the Muslim Brotherhood, and committed itself to the re-creation of the caliphate, abolished in 1924 by Mustafa Kemal. As an ideological party banned in most of the Muslim world, HT used to target expatriate Arabs in London but this shifted to recruiting young Muslims from across the country with South Asian backgrounds.[24]

HT were able to capitalize on anti-Saudi sentiment during the first Gulf war. Its 'polemical tabloid style' excited Muslim students who were not only 'looking for easy answers' to Western double standards in foreign policy but were also dissatisfied with the Saudi petro-dollar Salafi Islam, which was making inroads with the first returnee graduates from Medina University to Britain coming onstream. 'Often squeezed between the Salafis and HT, Muslim students were left with few alternatives to a crude, de-spiritualised, angry and self-righteous take on Islam'. The British '*ulama* – custodians of traditional Sunni Islam – were unable 'to develop a plausible alternative to ... [such] controversies'.

More worrying, such radical Islamist activity became a Trojan horse, allowing the unseen entry of a small but deadly group of violent jihadis – those whom Hamza Yusuf dubbed radical extremists. 'A combination of official silence and tacit Muslim approval allowed the jihadi involvement of British Muslims in Afghanistan in the late 1980s, and Bosnia and then Chechnya in the 1990s, to establish itself so long as the enemy was politically halal'. Birt means that so long as Usama bin Laden and the estimated 20,000 other 'Arab Afghans' – including the likes of Abu Hamza al-Misri – were fighting the Soviets, Western governments, along with Pakistan and Saudi Arabia, were happy to fund and lionize them as respected fighters of jihad. This changed, of course, when the Soviets were defeated and Al Qaeda turned its ire against the Saudi government for allowing infidel armies onto Saudi soil during the first Iraq war.

Birt concludes that the situation on campus has been exacerbated by the failure of the National Union of Students (NUS) to build 'proper alliances with Muslim students to tackle the tensions created by HT and others'. The NUS 'has effectively stigmatised a whole faith community'. He also blames the Union of Jewish Students and the pro-Israel lobby, which, he alleges, is too ready to conflate principled and informed anti-Zionist protest with anti-Semitism. In general, there is an absence of trust between student organizations which disables rational political debate. Instead, accusations of anti-Semitism or Islamophobia poison the atmosphere.[25]

A third theme to which *Q-News* often returns is that of alienation of sections of Muslim youth from its own community and the wider society. Fuad Nahdi's comments on the popularity of Abu Hamza al-Misri is one expression of this concern. Another is an article by Faisal Bodi, also pre-9/11, where he reflects on the world of 'Ali G', a popular TV creation by a British comedian and satirist modelled on nominally Muslim young men:

> *We laugh along with him because he is everything we do not wish our kids to be yet see evidence of daily ... The species of nominal Muslim Ali G is meant to represent [is] typically unemployed*

> *and poorly educated, he is the type who sees a brighter future in taking on the trappings of the LA 'gangsta' rather than the uncool and 'foreign' traditions of his parents. The sovereigns, the Tommy Hillfiger 'condom' hat, the goatee beard and the glasses all mark him out as that breed of young British Muslim whose idea of getting down has more to do with the dance floor than the prayer mat ... He is Muslim only by birth and can barely conceive of his religion in any orthodox sense ... His uncle Jamal, we are told in an interview with a feminist, is trisexual, 'he'll try anything' ... [he himself] will sleep with anyone; and he enjoys intimate relations with his girlfriend 'Julie'. The character gives the lie to the sound bite that Islam is Britain's fastest growing religion ... The British Muslim community is haemorrhaging ... the urban rude boy [demonstrates this].*[26]

The phenomenon of the urban rude boy, which has migrated from the USA to the UK, is clearly no longer confined to young black and white Britons. Bodi considers that it has had its greatest impact on young Muslims of Pakistani and Somali ancestry. As for what might be done, Yahya Birt locates the issues within the wider context of a crisis in masculinity affecting young Muslims as well as other communities.

In his reflection 'True and False Masculinity', he renders accessible the models and norms taken from classical Islamic views of manliness and chivalry, which reflect a Sufi pattern of self-scrutiny. These generate much sensible advice. Parents and community elders are urged to avoid 'self-righteous disdain or, even worse, indifference' and to embody 'patience and gentleness in counselling towards repentance' and thereby making possible a new start. Some practical measures are also identified: to lobby the governments of Afghanistan, Morocco and Turkey to crack down on drug production; to provide spaces where the problems of criminality and drug dealing and drug use are openly discussed and addressed; to develop Muslim-run youth and sports facilities; to appoint English-speaking imams as a matter of priority and 'to conduct as many programmes as possible in English which deal directly with issues facing young Muslims today' and create 'a full and relevant curriculum up to at least the age of sixteen by forging a strong partnership between the *ulama*, the mosque committee and the community'. Government is urged to provide extra funds to support Muslim voluntary organizations. And 'as a community we have to drop theological and legal differences from the [Indian] sub-continent to work together for the common good'.[27]

While *Q-News* continues to publish good investigative and critical journalism, by extending its reach to include Muslims in the USA and Canada it has begun to provide a forum for constructive voices, whether traditional or progressive, to encourage British Muslims to a more confident engagement with Western society in all its complexity. Recent issues have profiled Isla Rosser-Owen, who has initiated an online discussion forum for aspiring and established Muslim writers, poets, playwrights and those interested in literary pursuits (<www.qalamonline.com>); Bishop David Gillett, the chair of the recently launched national Christian–Muslim Forum; and Shami Chakrabarti of Liberty. Chakrabarti reflects on the implications of the Law Lords' ruling that the indefinite detention of foreign nationals under the 2001 Anti-Terrorism, Crime and Security Act is contrary to their human rights.

With regard to foregrounding the work of serious Islamic scholars, three, in particular, indicate the range of personalities and their concerns. Hasan Le-Gai Eaton, an English scholar, argues that traditional *fiqh* (Islamic jurisprudence), developed a thousand years ago, is silent on a range of issues which exercise contemporary Muslims, for example genetic engineering. He concludes that 'for centuries the good Muslim had no occasion to consult his or her conscience and perhaps consciences atrophied. Today there are no cut-and-dried answers and there has to be a rebirth of conscience'.[28] Mustafa Ceric, the Grand Mufti of Bosnia-Herzegovina, throws down the gauntlet to a new generation: 'it is now time that we in Europe offer ... an alternative interpretation of Islam [to that of Saudi Arabia and South Asia?] that would lead to creativity that is recognisable as Islamic-European and European Islamic ... that is not in the way of isolation, nor in the way of assimilation, but in the way of equal cultural interaction and civilisational cooperation'.[29]

A third scholar profiled is Habib Ali al-Jifri, heir of a scholarly Yemeni tradition rooted in Sufism. Habib Ali is director of the Tabah Foundation, a UAE-based think-tank and research centre. He was particularly active as a go-between in the recent Danish cartoons controversy, travelling to Denmark and Britain. While acknowledging legitimate Muslim anger with the cartoons and aspects of Western foreign policy, Habib Ali also points out that 'anger is no excuse for ignorance of our principles and our way of life'. Indeed, to seek to defend the prophet's honour without embodying his patience and forbearance is to betray him:

> *The Prophet is not alive in people's hearts, he's not alive in their spiritual wayfaring or in the way they do things and even in the way they list their priorities, and how they deal with others around them. That is what we're missing, this is the real problem.*[30]

We might characterize the concerns of each of these three Islamic thinkers as an appeal respectively to conscience, creativity and compassion.

Learning to be a Muslim youth worker

Muslim youth workers often find themselves, almost by default, as confidants of young people on religious issues. However, very few feel equal to such a role. They often have to negotiate a path between the secular ethos of much of the state-funded provision and the ideology of self-consciously Islamic movements. The Muslim Youthwork Foundation (MYF) was created in 2006 to enable them to navigate these worlds more confidently.

MYF is the fruit of research by M. G. Khan, a lecturer at Birmingham University, who trains youth, community and play workers. Its rationale was developed in the course of two national conferences held in Birmingham and Bradford, as well as a workshop on Muslim youth work. The former attracted five hundred delegates, two-thirds of whom were Muslim. A selection of papers prepared and delivered for these events have been published in a special issue of the in-house journal of the National Youth Agency, *Youth and Policy*, dedicated to Muslim youth work.[31]

The basic concern of MYF is to 'create safe spaces for young Muslim people to explore personal, social, spiritual and political choices'. The emphasis on 'exploration' is, of course, the same priority for Muslim educators identified by Dr Sahin, whose research on identity formation among Muslim students in Birmingham was mentioned in the previous chapter.

The declared purposes of MYF include the need to generate and connect critical thinking to youth work policy and practice; provide a platform that connects the voices of young people and youth workers to policy and government; and provide support and expertise to organizations seeking to develop such youth work. MYF's concern is to be inclusive – it exists for all young people who define themselves as Muslim – and non-sectarian – this is expanded to insist that its work be led by social realities rather than dogma – and young people themselves are integral to its leadership, development and project work. It seeks to respond to the lived experience of young people rather than to external events. In short, it seeks to help policy-makers get away from seeing young Muslims solely in terms of security problems.

The twelve members of the MYF board reflects the ethnic diversity of Muslim communities, including four women amongst whom is Shareefa Fulat, director of the Muslim Youth Helpline, and four academics from Birmingham and Leeds University, and encompass a range of skills from counselling, social work and conflict resolution to youth work proper. Members are drawn from across the country, with Birmingham, Bradford–Leeds and London well represented. One unique feature of the MYF board is its desire 'to integrate Muslim and non-Muslim youth work expertise, across age, faith, gender and this is reflected in … [three members who] have national roles/expertise from Christian, Jewish and secular traditions'.

Its two full-time staff are both young Muslim women, one of whom introduces herself as bringing to MYF 'a sense of creativity … I like to be quirky and inventive, to step outside the box, to dance around inside the box and at other times set fire to the damn box!' Creativity seems a feature of MYF as witnessed by its ambitious programme to provide resources for and to encourage local initiatives through a developing pool of trainers whose expertise ranges from understanding 'Rap' culture, through African drumming, to the psychology of football.

Their website flags up a range of activities and opportunities for young people including a site called 'Faces and Places', which allows young Muslims to use visual communication rather than words to explore identity, involving issues of 'exclusion, belonging, discrimination, religion, ethnic heritage and foreign policy' – in general, 'to tackle stereotypes which have been created about young Muslim people'. The initiative aims to increase involvement in arts and culture and to be a shop window for young Muslim talent in these fields. While itself non-sectarian, there are links to a range of Muslim organizations which encompass the full range of Islamic expression – Sunnis, whether Sufi, Salafi or Islamist, as well as Shia – along with Muslim associations for environmental issues, social sciences and human rights. Only the radical political fringe is excluded.

To read the background papers that led to the establishment of the MYF is to realize the daunting intellectual task the MYF has set itself. Jonathan Roberts, a Principal Lecturer on Youth Work at the University of Teeside – the board member who has had experience of Church youth work – remarked, in his response as a participant of the national conferences, that much of the current literature on youth work is based on 'the themes of race, gender and tackling inequality' but was silent on the 'subtleties of identity, culture and the consequences for young Muslims'.[32]

Roberts particularly valued the contribution from two Muslim speakers, one a German, Halima Krausen, the other, the Egyptian–Swiss Tariq Ramadan. The former argued that Islam could contribute something 'other than the polarised positions of idealizing the eastern tradition or being absorbed utterly in the western lifestyle'. She recommended space to return to the Islamic sources and think again; space to allow for reflection, discovery and self-education, including the ability to make mistakes! Ramadan was able to challenge misperceptions about Islamic law, which he understood as a straight path to ideals of justice and integrity rather than a preoccupation with draconian penal laws. He expressed the need for Muslim role models to bridge the gap between the mosques and the street. Roberts concluded that mainstream youth work had to make room for debating and embodying such perspectives and practices.

Another contribution by a Mancunian youth worker and researcher, Sadek Hamid, focuses on the tensions evident between 'Muslim' and 'Islamic' youth work. The latter is confessional, motivated by the desire to reach out to young people with the message of Islam. Like Christian evangelical outreach, the stated aim is for young people to return to and practise their faith. This he contrasts with 'Muslim' youth work, 'a person centred approach which starts with where the young person is at ... It is dialogical and facilitates self-discovery and empowerment. It assumes the young person has pressing needs that require immediate attention but [its] style of delivery and ethos is informed by and sensitive to the values of Islam'.[33]

Hamid has experienced at first hand the plethora of reformist Islamic youth movements in Britain, whose parent bodies are either the Muslim Brotherhood, in the Arab world, or Jama'at-i Islami, on the Indian subcontinent. He mentions a range of such movements, for example Young Muslims (YM), which has been in existence for over twenty years. Young Muslims caters for the 13–21 age group, has a separate girls' section, and provides study circles, lecture programmes, annual camps and sports competitions. It also produces a magazine,

Trends, as well as music cassettes and audio materials explaining aspects of Islam. In brief, it attempts to provide a 'counter-culture' for Muslim youth by producing a range of activities and media and alternatives to popular secular youth pastimes. Its members often run annual Ramadan radio stations in cities where they have a significant presence, such as Glasgow, Bradford and London. Young Muslims has recently formed the Islamic scouts group, which provides a way in to YM, and after graduating from YM members are expected to join the Islamic Society of Britain.

Hamid respects much of the work that groups such as YM have done. However, he has substantive criticisms. Young people's needs are often 'an appendage to achieving the organization's overall aims'. YM has the characteristics of many 'political vanguard movements' – inspired organizationally by the communists in the 1920s and 1930s – which saw themselves as charged by history to lead the masses but were usually out of touch with the day-to-day problems of those they would attract.[34] They tend to be elitist, recruiting from college and university students. Their pattern of 'ideological indoctrination' presents other groups as 'competitors', prevents co-operation and produces an 'insular mentality' which inhibits personal growth.

Few of their members have youth work skills and many are oblivious 'to wider social trends and changes taking place in mainstream youth culture'. There is an inability to accept 'constructive criticism' and they remain accountable only to the organizational hierarchy. Hamid's critique was developed both through personal involvement and research into such movements, including research into many ex-members, some of whom claim to have been 'actually harmed' by this type of youth work.

He acknowledges that latterly some of these organizations are 'belatedly' recognizing the importance of social welfare work and some members go on to train as youth, drugs and social workers. But the challenge remains of their relevance to young people and their willingness to serve them without hoping that they will become workers in a movement. In summary, Hamid considers that if such groups are to engage with all kinds of Muslim youth, 'they have to move beyond the narrow ideological and methodological approaches that arise out of sectarian trends imported by the first generation'.[35]

Another difficult set of issues turns on the desirability or otherwise of girls-only youth work. The dilemmas here are sharply posed in a paper by another lecturer at Birmingham University, who also is part of the MYF board. Gill Cressey's reflections are rooted in personal work and research with Muslim girls in Birmingham. She rehearses the contents of a recent Friday mosque sermon delivered to students by a young imam, who urged 'Brothers, sisters and elders' to 'live together as brothers [*sic*]'. He continued to pray for 'the young people and women to be corrected from evil and guided to goodness'.[36]

Cressey points to a number of difficult tensions. 'Islam accepts that there should be no compulsion in religion on the one hand and gives parents the duty to discipline their children if they do not pray on the other hand'. She cites the comments of a Muslim girl:

> *I'd rather go to mixed youth activities so I can learn how to mix sensibly without a big issue over it, after all if I want to work and earn and survive or go to Uni and all that I have to learn to mix confidently.*

Cressey then quite properly asks:

> *Are we trying to socialise young women into existing roles perpetuating control over them by men and by elders or supporting their development by offering a space to be themselves and to make life choices of their own?*

When considering the case for separate provision, she rightly remarks:

> *Separation should not be confused with control and subordination. It is the nature of the space allocated to young Muslim women that is important regarding whether the space is controlling or liberating, a place to feel safe, at home, valued and accepted or a place to feel restricted and contained.*[37]

M. G. Khan's foundation document for MYF is alert to many of the tensions which attend this new venture. He wryly comments that reporters from two youth work magazines who attended the first conference in Birmingham did not write it up despite the presence of key thinkers, policy-makers and religious leaders. Only six months later was he asked to write a piece for one of the magazines ... on the anniversary of 7/7. 'This only seemed to confirm the view that it is [negative] events that allow issues related to Muslim young people to enter into the public domain.'[38]

Youth work, like many other professions, has been slow to respond to the specific needs of Muslim young people. A secular approach to youth work can unwittingly exclude Islam when dealing with 'the socio-economic consequences of young people's "Muslimness"'. Too often, 'the self-representation by Muslim young people as Muslims remains largely unrecognised by a profession that claims that its starting point is where the young person is at'.[39] This reinforces the point which Roberts has made on the invisibility of Muslim texts and contexts to mainstream youth providers.

Khan hopes that MYF will encourage Muslim youth work which can provide 'interventions in a crucial ... space outside the home, mosque and school', thus meeting Ramadan's desideratum for Muslim role models to bridge the gap between mosque and street. Further, such Muslim youth work could help young men and women to be taken seriously in the Muslim community. It might also begin to address 'the gendered nature of the representational sphere in the Muslim context'. Khan is clear that 'in the arts field Muslims are still at a point at which they are justifying their right to use the medium'.[40]

Khan is clear that too often Muslim youth workers and youth work have been reactive, with little chance 'to present its own voice and distinctive shape'. In a telling phrase he argues that such youth work has become a 'condom' that can provide 'safe' entry into the lives of young people to satisfy immediate policy imperatives. The challenge is to move from reactive consultation to structured collaboration.[41]

A citizenship course for mosques

In May 2007 the Bradford Council for Mosques (BCM) launched a beautifully produced course on practical citizenship – Nasiha. Nasiha, an Arabic word for 'good counsel' or 'sincere advice', is the brainchild of a young teacher, 'Asif' (not his real name), active in a local mosque committee.[42] Asif, who embodies the generous Islamic humanism of one of his mentors, Shaikh Hamza Yusuf, teaches in a local school with a majority of Muslim pupils. Since 9/11 he has worried about the attitudes of some youngsters with regard to three issues. First, there is a temptation to lionize Usama bin Laden as a sort of Robin Hood figure who stands up to the contemporary equivalent of the arrogant tyrant, the sheriff of Nottingham; but they lack any real knowledge of the extent to which his extremism is a betrayal of Islamic norms. Secondly, the complexities of rival nationalisms involved in the Israel–Palestine tragedy is oversimplified as Muslim versus Jew, which fuels a casual anti-Semitism. Finally, traditional Islamic formation in the *madrasa* often does not equip youngsters with knowledge relevant to their situation in Britain today. When they look outside the mosque for teaching, they often find themselves exposed to radical websites and materials which present the 'British Muslim' as an oxymoron. This prevents them from acknowledging and valuing the positive aspects of British society.

Nasiha is a bold attempt to work these insights into a course on citizenship for 12- to 16-year-olds. Asif identifies the themes and Muslim scholars from the main schools of thought, Sunni and Shia, illustrate the materials with appropriate texts. The intention is to pilot the materials in a number of mosques in Bradford, where imams will be given appropriate support and mentoring to work through the materials. At the end of the course they will be given a certificate which indicates that they have successfully delivered the course and achieved competence in a number of areas: the English language; child protection policy; knowledge of relevant aspects of British society, such as appropriate general legal issues, the British political system, and the culture of tolerance and free speech; as well as how to promote a healthy and safe environment for education, and foster a common sense of belonging informed by the specifics of Islamic teachings on citizenship and its supporting values which contribute to the common good.

The course is accompanied by additional materials, available on a website, by scholars from within each of the major Islamic traditions.[43] These enhance the confidence of those users who would locate themselves within one of these particular traditions. Along with the professionally produced course work – illustrated with some arresting examples of Islamic calligraphy – they provide an invaluable resource for teachers in state schools, who now have materials to address contentious and difficult issues. Such a project also has the potential additional benefit of furthering positive links between mosques and local schools, which could be mutually reinforcing. Too often the relationship has been one of mutual suspicion and ignorance.

The student in the mosque who completes the course will also be awarded a certificate which lists the units covered. These include a core of compulsory modules and additional subjects from which the pupils can select a favourite topic. The compulsory modules explore issues of the sanctity of life, respect for teachers, parenting, the distinction between legitimate and illegitimate ways of earning a living, anti-social behaviour, 'Good Muslim, Good Citizen', elections, respect and tolerance, good and bad company, and anger management. The additional topics cover such issues as the environment, volunteering and aspects of Islamic history. The two history topics draw on case studies within Europe where interfaith and inter-community relations were frequently constructive, namely Andalusia and the Ottoman Empire.

The format of the lessons is an interesting hybrid of school and *madrasa* teaching styles. Each lesson includes stated objectives, key words, supporting material drawn from the Qur'an and the Prophet's life, lessons learned, activities/scenarios, concluding with homework. For example, a lesson entitled 'Oath of Peace' lists the objectives: to understand what kind of citizen a Muslim should be as explained by the Prophet; to learn that as UK citizens Muslims have a fundamental responsibility to respect British laws and to identify the UK as their home and to take responsibility for establishing peace and harmony. Key words include oath, peace, justice, trust, respect and responsibility.

Pertinent Qur'anic verses follow and episodes from the Prophet's life drive home the message. Under 'Activities' the student is asked to write about the harmful consequences of 7/7 as they affect: the families of the victims (Muslim and non-Muslim); community relations; Muslim businesses; Muslim women wearing the *hijab*; young Muslims applying for jobs. They are then asked to explain how the selected Qur'anic and Prophetic material might inform their answers.

The scenarios chosen are also to the point, as this example shows:

> *Ahmad is 14 years old and is a Pakistani citizen, who obtains a visa to come to England. When he arrives in the UK, he makes friends with Muslims who are British citizens, and who say they are fighting jihad against the UK. They are planning to harm people and property in the name of Islam .. [They] decide to target the local Asda store. The manager has a family and three children. He is a Christian and was part of the 'Stop the War Campaign', and worked with Muslims. 'No soul shall bear another's burden' is the teaching of the Qur'an. Is the Manager responsible for people losing their lives outside his country when he has been against the war? What should Ahmad do when he knows what his religious friends are going to do? Is it right to take innocent people's lives? What does Islam teach us? Who will suffer if this religious group carries out their action? What advice should Ahmad give them?*

The activities and scenarios resonate with the experience of many young Muslims. The Qur'anic and Prophetic material chosen to illustrate the topics is frequently challenging. In the lesson on 'Good Muslim, Good Citizen' the following Qur'anic verse is cited in the context of the need to oppose injustice: 'O believers! Stand firmly for justice, giving witness for Allah, even though it be against yourselves, your parents or your relations, or against whom you are a witness (whether the man be rich or poor)' (4.135).

In the lesson on the sanctity of human life the material categorically states that suicide bombing is not permitted and that 'jihad is not about causing havoc and loss of life, or damage to property, or injecting fear into the communities. Such actions are outside the fold of Islamic law and distort people's perceptions of the Islamic faith.'

Similar points are made in the material on avoiding groups 'preaching hatred and harm'. The scenarios chosen drive the lessons home:

> *Fraz is working in Morrisons with his friend Ukasha. Fraz does not like any person who buys alcohol. Is his hatred Islamically justified?*
>
> *Yasin is on his way home when he bumps into a group on the street. The group gives him a leaflet on which is written, 'The UK hates Islam'. He listens to their conversation and they talk to him about how the West has killed so many innocent Muslims . . . This group is trying to make Muslims hate non-Muslims. Is this what the Prophet taught us?*

Again a pertinent Qur'anic quotation is provided: 'Let not enmity of any people incite you not to do justice. Do justice: that is nearer to piety' (5.8).

The lesson on 'Respect and Tolerance' includes as homework examples of how Muslims have learnt from other communities. A tradition of a gracious encounter between an Arab Jew and the Prophet is cited to indicate the propriety of praying for non-Muslims and respecting them. A number of Qur'anic verses are quoted to support the view that God recognizes cultural and ethnic diversity, as well as the freedom to believe in other faiths: 'There is no compulsion in religion' (2.256), 'For you is your religion and for me is mine' (109.6), 'And if your Lord had so willed, He could surely have made all mankind a single community' (11.118), and the verse which indicates that humankind was created as different nations and tribes 'so that you might get to know one another' (49.13). This latter verse presents diversity as God-given and to be respected rather than obliterated.

In the lesson on volunteering and participation in elections plenty of material is cited which justifies both. In a context where many Wahhabis/Salafis and the radical fringe – Hizb ut-Tahrir and al Muhajirun – have traditionally opposed participation in democratic politics, this material is a clarion call for involvement. The section on homework includes finding out about Muslim charities and whether any have 'worked with Christian charities on certain projects'.

The scenarios chosen to illustrate what counts as earning an honest living provide a sad commentary on the temptations to which urban youth of all communities are exposed:

> *Ahmad is at school, talking to David, who explains that he wants to be an electrician when he grows up. Ahmad is not interested, he thinks he can become rich by selling drugs. Who is closer to the Prophet's teaching?*
>
> *Jamil buys a car which has done 110,000 miles and decides to 'clock it back' to 35,000 miles, then sell it. He makes a profit of £2000. Is it lawful/halal . . . explain.*
>
> *Raheel meets a van driver on the street who is selling computers for £20. Should he enquire where the man got the items from . . . ?*

The Bradford Council for Mosques is to be commended for supporting this bold initiative. On the student's achievement certificate are the words: 'the resources and materials used have been accredited by eminent scholars from different Islamic traditions'. The initiative represents a creative partnership between a young imaginative teacher, the '*ulama*, the BCM and a range of funding bodies. It offers a welcome example of how traditional Islamic scholarship can be quarried to inform a range of contentious issues. It could also serve to chip away at the wall of suspicion between school and mosque.

Notes

1. The comments in these two paragraphs are informed by a conversation I had over a meal in London with both Asim, the present chairman of City Circle, and Yahya Birt, recently appointed its first director (15 December 2006), as well as a range of illuminating material on their website <www.thecitycircle.com>. There is also a useful short article by Konrad Pedziwiatr, 'New Muslim Elites in the City', in *ISIM Review*, 18 (22 September 2006), pp. 24–5.

2. Delivered to the Fabian Society's conference on 14 January 2006 on 'Who Do We Want To Be? The Future of Britishness'. Available on the City Circle website.

3. 'About Us: City Circle Piece for the Fabian Society', available on the City Circle website.

4. 'City Circle Projects', available ibid.

5. The Christian scholar Jaroslav Pelikan is credited with this epigram. See V. Hotchkiss and P. Henry (eds), *Orthodoxy and Western Culture* (Crestwood, NY: St Vladimir's Seminary Press, 2005), p. 176.

6. 'City Circle Values – Chairman's Address to iftari Event, 22 October 2005', available on the City Centre Website.

7. Madeleine Bunting deservedly won the Race in the Media Award in June 2005 for her 'Young Muslim and British Project', which came to fruition in the book she edited, *Islam, Race and Being British* (London: The *Guardian* in association with Barrow Cadbury Trust, 2005).

8. See *Arab Human Development Report* (New York: United Nations, 2003), p. 67.

9. 'Past Events: Cultural jihad, 17 November 2006', available on the City Circle website.

10. M. Bright, *When Progressives Treat with Reactionaries: The British State's Flirtation with Radical Islamism* (London: Policy Exchange, 2006), pp. 7–8.

11. This was evident in the membership of the seven Muslim working groups the government assembled after 7/7 comprising the Preventing Extremism Together initiative, PET.

12. R. P. Mitchell, *The Society of the Muslim Brothers* (New York: Oxford University Press, 1993 edn), p. 216.

13. J. Sacks, *Will We Have Jewish Grandchildren?* (Ilford, Essex: Vallentine Mitchell, 1994), p. 83.

14. F. Nahdi, 'Doublespeak: Islam and the Media', available at <www. OpenDemocracy.net>.

15. *Q-News*, 11–24 October 1996, p. 16.

16. *Q-News*, March 2004, p. 25.

17. *Q-News*, 26 July–1 August 1996, p. 5.

18. *Q-News*, February 1999, p. 27.

19. Ibid., p. 24.

20. *Q-News*, October 2001, p. 14.

21. R. Aslam, *No God But God: The Origins, Evolution and Future of Islam* (London: Arrow Books, 2006), p. 133.

22. *Q-News*, October 2001, p. 15.

23. Y. Birt, 'Fear and Loathing on Campus', *Q-News*, July–August 2002, pp. 24–6.

24. I have documented how they cynically swooped into Bradford and held meetings after a riot in a Pakistani area of the city in 1995. See my 'British Muslims and the Search for Religious Guidance', in John R. Hinnells (ed.), *The Religious Reconstruction in the South Asian Diasporas* (London: PalgraveMacmillan, 2007).

25. *Q-News*, July–August 2002, pp. 24–6.

26. *Q-News*, February 2000, p. 31.

27. *Q-News*, November 2000, pp. 19–21.

28. *Q-News*, October 2003, p. 48.

29. *Q-News*, March 2004, p. 20.

30. *Q-News*, May 2006, pp. 37–41.

31. See *Youth and Policy*, 92 (Summer 2006). The key address – 'Towards a

National Strategy for Muslim Youth Work' by M. G. Khan – is accessible on the MYF website as well as in this issue of *Youth and Policy*. Unless otherwise stated, all information on the MYF is taken from its website, <www.muslimyouthworkfoundation.org>, last accessed 28 March 2007.

32. J. Roberts, 'Making a Place for Muslim Youth Work in British Youth Work', *Youth and Policy*, 92 (Summer 2006), p. 20.

33. S. Hamid, 'Models of Muslim Youth Work: Between Reform and Empowerment', *Youth and Policy*, 92 (2006), pp. 82–3.

34. The best study of Jama'at-i Islami in Pakistan is S. V. R. Nasr, *The Vanguard of the Islamic Revolution* (London: I. B. Tauris, 1994).

35. Hamid, 'Models of Muslim Youth Work', pp. 86–7.

36. Gill Cressey, 'Muslim Girlswork: The Ultimate Separatist Cage?', *Youth and Policy*, 92 (2006), pp. 33–4.

37. Ibid., pp. 37, 40.

38. M. G. Khan, 'Towards a National Strategy for Muslim Youth Work', *Youth and Policy*, p. 11.

39. Ibid.

40. Ibid.

41. Ibid., pp. 17, 13.

42. I have preserved the anonymity of 'Asif', a friend of mine, to spare him embarrassment. The huge amount of work he put into the project was done to serve God and humankind rather than for self-publicity. I am grateful to him for furnishing me with a copy of Nasiha in advance of its official launch. All quotations are taken from this document, which is unpaginated.

43. See <www.nasiha.co.uk>.

CHAPTER 4

Only Connect: Can the *'ulama* Address the Crisis in the Transmission of Islam to Young British Muslims?

For the last few years, the cream of a new generation of English-educated *'ulama*, schooled at Bury in the mother house of a network of 'seminaries' established in the UK, have met each summer at Kidderminster. At this attractive rural location, they participate in a conference for young men. This represents the major public interface between the Deobandi imams and British Muslim youth. Most of the *'ulama* are of Gujarati ethnicity and many are also the spiritual disciples of the founder and principal of Bury, Sheikh Yusuf Motala.

Over three days, they deliver addresses on a variety of topics to an audience aged between 15 and 30 years, numbering a couple of thousand. The most recent conference included presentations on the miracle of the Qur'an, remembrance of Allah, the reality of faith, repentance, love of the Prophet, Islam's contribution to humanity, and practical issues such as health and Islam, what counts as true success, the importance of education, and Muslims in Europe.[1]

However, what is striking is an evident tension in many of the talks between those who are urging a wide-ranging engagement with non-Muslim society and those who seem content to keep their spatial, social and intellectual distance from an infidel (*kufr*) society, often painted in lurid colours. The difference is seen most clearly if we compare two talks delivered in 2002, one by Mahmood Chandia, the other by Riyadhul Haq.[2] Both were trained at Bury, and both subsequently gained degrees in Cairo from Sunni Islam's most venerable centre of traditional Islam, Azhar.

Mahmood's presentation points to the necessity for Britain's youthful Muslim population to consider the importance of education. He insists that if they are to have influence in society they must raise their educational aspirations, for only thus will they be able to recapture that time in medieval Spain where they co-existed creatively with Christians and Jews and made significant additions to the store of knowledge across many disciplines. Time and again he repeats that historically Muslims integrated but did not assimilate. The respect in which they were held turned on the pen, not the sword. He regrets that, along with other ethnic minorities in Britain, so few Muslims go into education and teaching – the figure for all ethnic minorities is 4 per cent compared to 25 per cent in IT and 10–12 per cent in medicine.

A good education is presented as a passport to influence in the key professions that shape the nature of society: academia, law, politics, civil service and the media. Muslims are urged to engage in all these areas not simply out of narrow sectional Muslim interests – 'because it serves our needs' – but in 'the interests of wider society'.

He then worries about attitudes in the Muslim communities. He remarks that many students do not complete their examinations in science, medicine, law or journalism and use the 'excuse' that they had to give priority instead to revivalist tours. Mahmood is scathing about such attitudes. The Spanish experience is presented as teaching the important lesson that Muslims adopted a balanced attitude with regard to secular and religious learning and sought to contribute to the common good. He notices that because Muslim students 'do not know how to handle that freedom they enjoy on the university campus, [their] rate of drop outs ... is highest [amongst all communities] and still rising'.

Mahmood remarks that the most popular disciplines in university are politics, philosophy, economics and law and the number one students are from the Jewish community. He then asks rhetorically: 'What of Muslims? Not interested in politics ... philosophy? ... [We] do not know what the word means ... economics? ... [No need for that.] I have my corner shop and petrol station ... law? I make up my own rules'. Mahmood attacks the complacency and low educational aspirations of many within the Muslim communities. He points out that there is an open door in British society to influence its future shape but only if they engage at every level, whether as school governors, academics or journalists.

Riyadhul Haq's talk, 'Steadfastness in the Days of *fitna* [discord]', suggests another set of attitudes. He has no truck with the 'propaganda' that all has changed since 9/11:

> *Nothing has really changed. The persecution of the Muslims … enmity, hostility, hatred of the* umma … *ridicule and vilification of Islam [is] part of a constant battle between* haqq *and* batil, *truth and falsehood, which did not start on 9/11 but [was] present from the beginning [of Islam].*

He argues that such discord was promised by Allah as a test to his people. A number of supporting prophetic traditions are cited to the effect that a time would come when men would prefer to be in the grave rather than alive; that to be steadfast in their faith would be like holding fast 'to a burning cinder'. Muslims stand 'in awe of US fire power and economic might … their technology … [enabling] them to spy on the whole globe and [seemingly] bomb anywhere at will … [as well as] their culture of McDonald's … their fashions, music … their apparent liberty and democracy'. They have even begun to 'doubt the Word of Allah and the supremacy of Islam over all other faiths, cultures and ways of life'. Faced with the Western world's 'blind passion for retaliation' post-9/11 some Muslims have begun to change their names and avoid dressing according to the *Sunna* (Prophetic custom) and want to dissolve into wider society, 'Not just out of fear but doubt about the truth of Allah's promises when they see non-Muslims straddling the globe.'

This jeremiad continues with stirring stories of exemplary Muslims standing up to the superpowers of their day. The Prophet himself was not spared such hardships in the Battle of the Trench but prevailed. When he prophesied that the wealth and glory of Abyssinia, Rome and Persia would fall to Islam he was mocked by the doubters and hypocrites. He did not see it come to pass but it did.

Riyadhul Haq seeks to reassure Muslims that Allah has not abandoned his community. He has promised that they will know glory, liberty and liberation. However 'demoralised and divided and doubting', Allah will reward their steadfastness and patience. In brief, Muslims must not despair: 'Allah's light will not be extinguished … Allah's truth and guidance are such that "His religion will prevail over all other religions … [even though] the *mushrikin* [those who 'associate' a creature with the Creator] detest it".'[3]

This lachrymose reading of contemporary history is Manichaean. Reality is presented in terms of a familiar binary opposition. The undifferentiated *kuffar* (unbelievers) are depicted as intent on humiliating Muslims. No mention here of the more nuanced Qur'anic term for Christians and Jews – 'People of the Book'. Unlike Mahmood Chandia, there is little hint of self-criticism and integration is conflated with assimilation. *Contra* Chandia, such an essentialist vision does not provide space for Muslims to engage critically with and contribute to wider society. All in all, we have two starkly competing narratives. Riyadhul Haq, drawing on Qur'anic verses, Prophetic traditions and the early Islamic history of successful imperial conquests argues for perseverance which will be rewarded when Islam once again prevails. We will return later to these two rival narratives struggling for pre-eminence within an influential Islamic tradition, imported from South Asia.

This chapter will clarify the challenges facing the *'ulama* if they are to connect confidently with young British Muslims, and reflect on their status and training and the tasks they perform. I shall also highlight the activities of a few pioneers moving into new fields of work.

A mountain to climb: the work of generations?

As Muslims have travelled through and traded with new linguistic and cultural worlds they have always been confronted with new questions. As they have searched for religious guidance, they have generally turned to two categories of specialist: the Muslim jurists, who answer with legal opinions, or Sufis, custodians of experiential knowledge of God. This process has always generated a constant dialectic of adaptation to new societies and a process of 'Islamization', whereby *madrasa*-trained scholars ceaselessly campaign against

> *'aberrant' local custom ... whether referred to as reform (*islah*), renewal (*tajdid*), religious summoning (*da'wa*) or even holy struggle (*jihad*) ... to penetrate unfamiliar territory, to teach, cajole, inspire, and lead local peoples into a more 'proper' observance of the faith.*[4]

However, the challenges facing *'ulama* if they are to transmit Islam to a new generation of British-educated Muslims are daunting. First, they have to create institutions of Islamic formation – *dar al 'uloom* – in Britain which can generate a leadership able to connect socially, intellectually and linguistically with the 52 per cent of Muslims under 25 years of age, a majority of whom were born and educated in Britain, and whose first language is increasingly English rather than Arabic, Bengali or Urdu. Secondly, their monopoly as custodians of Islam has been challenged within the Middle East and South Asia for over a hundred years, initially by modernists and latterly by Islamists. Thirdly, they have to compete with the well-funded Saudi Wahhabi/Salafi tradition, which has exacerbated intra-Muslim sectarianism.[5] Fourthly, on university campuses they find themselves up against well-organized radical groups such as Hizb ut-Tahrir, the dynamics of which will be explored in the following chapter. All these groups have websites and it is thus possible to educate oneself outside the world of traditional religious leaders. To add to their difficulties such tasks have to be discharged now within the shadow of 9/11 and 7/7 amidst increasing media and security scrutiny.

If these challenges were not demanding enough, Muslim religious leaders who have come from Muslim majority countries such as Pakistan and Bangladesh have to re-adjust a formative (Sunni) intellectual tradition, articulated in a world where Muslims took power and dominance for granted, to a situation where they are a minority, in a context which entails the de-territorialization of Islam. The late Dr Zaki Badawi (d. 2006), the doyen of Muslim religious leaders in Britain, remarked almost a quarter a century ago that '[Sunni] Muslim theology offers, up to [now], no systematic formulations of being a minority'.[6]

Similarly, the compendium of Islamic law offers little guidance for those who have chosen to leave the Islamic world and live as a minority in non-Muslim society. Only recently has this begun to be addressed, with the creation of a European Council for Fatwa and Research (ECFR) formed in 1997 with headquarters in Dublin. ECFR has yet to establish its credentials. First, its president is the controversial Yusuf al-Qaradawi, the Qatar-based scholar and former member of the Muslim Brotherhood, who has sought to justify suicide bombing in Israel/Palestine as martyrdom operations. Further, its membership hardly reflects the ethnic makeup of British Muslim communities, as 30 of the current 39 members are drawn from the Arab world.[7]

The status of the *'ulama*

The category of *'ulama* refers to the products of traditional religious education. Writing of India, a historian notes that they were not

> *a hierarchy or an order; if they were a professional body, they were without . . . a registration council or a court of discipline . . . They did not possess equal qualifications or individual parity of esteem. Not much more than pretension united the product of one of the great teaching centres . . . and the village* mulla *who, though he could recite the Qur'an in Arabic, could hardly understand what he was reciting . . . As long as a man followed a traditional syllabus of study . . . and accepted the* ijma *[consensus] of his learned predecessors, he would be accepted as an* alim.[8]

New figures from the Foreign Office show that 420 imams from Pakistan have been granted visas to come to Britain to discharge religious duties since 1997.[9] This suggests that many mosque committees, dominated by the elders, still prefer to import religious personnel from their home country rather than employ English-educated *'ulama* now coming onstream. This despite the fact that of the two important theological schools (*maslak*) of South Asian Sunni Islam – the Deobandi and the Barelwis – the former has been particularly successful in developing a network of *madrasa* in Britain.

What is clear is that the social status of the majority of mosque imams is modest whether in South Asia or in Britain. He is an employee of the mosque committee. In rural Pakistan he is often funded by landlords, in Britain by businessmen.[10] Further, many imams are poorly paid, so the best educated in Britain often seek employment outside the mosque or eke out a living by doing additional part-time work. In Indo-Pakistan affluent Muslims hardly ever send their children to such institutions, which are considered as 'care for the poor'.[11] This perception is partly echoed in a survey of Muslim opinion in the UK about the *madrasa*. One interviewee pointed out that attendance at such institutions was often motivated more by socio-economic need than religion: 'it's a cheap education . . . and they get fed and looked after'.[12]

Not only do imams, especially from rural backgrounds, enjoy low status, but they do not automatically receive respect. A recent anthropological study of a Punjabi village noted that

> *There is respect for their position, but not for them. Stories of child abuse, alcoholism, illiteracy, financial corruption . . . are everywhere . . . In a survey [to elicit] who people asked to help them in their problems, not one respondent said that they would go to any of the local maulvis for any problem.*[13]

A majority of Pakistani people in times of trouble visit the local Sufi and his shrine – the heart of Barelwi Islam. Within this world, the imam is often derided as a bearer of bookish knowledge and sectarianism.[14] Such sectarianism has become the bane of Pakistan. The escalation of sectarian strife, whether Sunni–Shia – exacerbated by the Taliban in Afghanistan – or intra-Sunni, has been the focus of much recent academic commentary. The Pakistani state, in particular, has been accused of exacerbating such sectarianism by 'scaling up *antidemocratic* and *antipluralist* trends in society'.[15]

Nothing has been more damaging since General Zia's military tutelage of Pakistan (1977–88) than the progressive subversion of the Pakistani educational system by Islamic ideologies. According to a celebrated report by distinguished educationalists, early Pakistani textbooks presented ancient Hindu history without denigration, criticized aspects of the activities of early Muslim conquerors and acknowledged with gratitude Gandhi's role in saving many Muslims at partition. These expansive views have been replaced during the last thirty years by narrow, ideological readings which vilify and create hatred of the (especially Hindu) 'other' – while justifying violent jihad and glorifying martyrdom. All in all, this has contributed to the growing violence in Pakistani society, whether intra-sectarian or against religious and ethnic minorities, as well as women.[16]

It does not follow, of course, that these unflattering assessments of imams persist in Britain. However, recent studies by British Muslim intellectuals paint a somewhat dispiriting picture. Professor Ansari, in his history of Muslims in Britain, remarks dryly that the proliferation of mosques is 'accompanied by sectarian fragmentation and ideological inflexibility'.[17] A study which largely showcases the work of young British Muslim scholars barely mentions them at all.[18] This does not suggest they are considered central to the future of Muslim Britain.

The view depicted in the national press is hardly more encouraging. A young journalist on *The Times*, Burhan Wazir, a Glaswegian of Pakistani origins, concluded in one of a series of articles on British Muslims:

> *In the past six weeks ... leaders of Muslim organisations, Muslim parliamentarians, parents [stressed the] ... need [for] an educated clergy [*sic*] that speaks English and is erudite in the customs and conventions of the British Isles ... Fewer than 10 per cent of British*

> *imams have received their instruction in the UK . . . [Imams include] dictatorial part-timers . . . [recruited by] undemocratic councils . . . Typically imams have no employment contract, no pension and often no regular salary . . . a career marked by poverty is unlikely to tempt well-educated, British born Muslims away from commerce, medicine and information technology.*[19]

In *She Who Disputes*, a recent report by the Muslim Women's Network, the picture of imam and mosque is equally negative. While a few positive changes are acknowledged, the overall picture is of the mosque as a largely male space: in Leicester a survey suggested that less than 2 per cent of trustees on mosque committees were women.[20] Since male community leaders pay the imam's salary, he is presented as unable to address culturally taboo issues, such as domestic violence. Moreover, given the frequently tight-knit nature of communities served by local mosques, the women have little confidence that confidentiality will be respected.

There is also impatience with the content and teaching style of the imams. A Londoner is weary with some of the language used in the mosque: 'I used to hate the word "kaffir" (infidel) – everything that goes wrong is down to non-Muslims. We need to look at ourselves – and improve. We must respect other religions. This would help kids be better human beings.' A young woman from Manchester complains that in the mosque you are taught the Qur'an in Arabic. If this was done in English we could 'discuss it, learn from scholars, and be able to question what [we were] told'. Another from Birmingham comments sardonically that 'the men in the mosques are not going to tell anyone about women's rights under Islam! I had to go and get a book on Islam in English, to learn about my own religion!'

Exasperation is expressed that 'Muslim men sometimes think that they are born with the right to hit women and Muslim women think that it's religious'. A Birmingham woman notes that 'if khutbahs [sermons] in the mosque were made on the issue of women's rights, it would have an effect on the men who go there'. Unsurprisingly, some women complain of the dominance of conservative literature and want access to 'progressive interpretation on women and women's rights'.[21]

Such negative perceptions are the staple of many Muslim websites. The following comments from a chat room run by the Muslim Public Affairs Committee for the UK, organized by a couple of young British

Pakistani graduates, gives a fair sample: it is taken for granted that many imams simply come to Britain to get a passport and then leave to find a better-paid job; teaching methods are characterized by 'the stick not love'; local and national press items involving mosque disputes between rival *biradaris* disputing the appointment of the imam are posted; an article in the *Independent* is reproduced in its entirety, headed: 'Feud at Birmingham mosque is blamed for second murder'.[22]

Training of *'ulama*: the tradition explored

Professor Akbar Ahmed, after discussions with *madrasa* teachers and an examination of their syllabi over a period of twenty years, concluded that the typical institution was narrow and 'exclusively Islamic' – based on the Qur'an, the *Sunna* and *sharia* – and 'encouraged religious chauvinism':

> *[with no space for] non-Muslim philosophers or historians ... no Max Weber ... worse, even Muslim ones, like Ibn Khaldun ... [were] missing ... [All in all, they embodied an] Islam minus its sophisticated legacy of art, culture, mysticism, and philosophy.*[23]

The seminal studies of Muhammad Zaman – a specialist on classical Islam and the social and intellectual world of contemporary Indo-Pakistani *madrasa* – do not challenge Ahmed's general point. However, they offer a more considered treatment of the potential for the Islamic disciplines – especially Islamic jurisprudence – to engage with some aspects of the modern world. Zaman is not impressed by attempts to classify neatly the Pakistani *'ulama* as either extremist or moderate, political or apolitical. This he illustrates in a telling example from the writings of one of Pakistan's most distinguished Deobandi *'ulama*, Maulana Taqi 'Uthmani, a former judge of the Shari'at Appellate Bench of the Supreme Court of Pakistan and vice-president of one of Pakistan's largest *madrasa* in Karachi.

While noting the 'studied ambiguity' of Islamic discourse and practice, not least the pragmatic politics of some *'ulama*, Zaman summarizes 'Uthmani's detailed answer to a question put to him about the legal status of 'aggressive' as opposed to 'defensive' jihad, both of which the questioner assumed to be redundant with regard to non-Muslim states which allowed Muslim minorities to proselytize:

> *['Uthmani] ... disputed the idea that opportunities for peaceful proselytism constituted sufficient grounds for regarding a non-Muslim*

> *state as friendly. The crucial issue is . . . the 'might' . . . of the non-Muslim state, which, being presently greater than that of Muslim states, is by itself an obstacle on the path to proselytism . . . It is this might that jihad seeks to undo . . . ['Uthmani expresses] contemptuous disdain for the view that the sort of expansionism aggressive jihad represents has no place in the modern world.*

Professor Zaman insists that 'Uthmani's position is a *theoretical* defence of the idea of jihad, rather than a call to arms:

> *His concern is to safeguard what he sees as Islam's* timeless verities *– including what the Qur'an or the Prophet's example has to say about jihad – against efforts to reinterpret or repackage Islam in the light of . . . liberal values . . . The real issue . . . seems to be that of defending jihad because it has all along been part of the Islamic juristic and historical tradition.*

Zaman observes that within Pakistan, any reform of the curriculum would have to engage with the reality that 'many Pakistani madrasa . . . maintain ties with militant sectarian organizations in the country . . . and the views of the 'ulama on such things as the position of women or on pluralism are often far from being conducive to a democratic society'.[24]

Zaman is raising a real problem. The women cited in the earlier report – *She Who Disputes* – assume a number of positions without argument, among them that what counts as Islamic rights for women is unproblematic, and similarly that respect and understanding of other religions is a given. However, as a scholar of the classical tradition, Zaman is aware that very different views are embedded in classical legal texts and revered compilations of Prophetic traditions, the mainstay of *madrasa* education. For example, a popular twelfth-century legal text, *Hidaya* (Guidance), takes for granted that in a range of legal cases 'the evidence required is of two men or of one man and two women'.[25] The formula 'one man equals two women' has been extrapolated from a Qur'anic verse dealing with a particular issue but now generalized to encompass most legal cases.

If we turn to an influential compilation of Prophetic traditions selected by Imam Nawawi, a Syrian scholar who died in 1278, entitled *Riyadh us Saliheen* (Garden of the Righteous), similar arguments are made. Traditions are cited which suggest that women are congenitally defective and should be considered by husbands 'as captives in your possession'; if they 'act licentiously in an open way, then leave them alone on their beds and beat them but not severely'. With regard to non-Muslims, the following tradition is cited: 'Do not initiate the greeting for the Jews and Christians. When you meet one of them in the road, force him to the narrowest part of it'. *Hidaya* continues to be an important component of legal training in Islamic 'seminaries' in Britain. Indeed, a new translation has just been published in England. The translations from *Riyadh us Saliheen* are those of a female scholar whose work appears on a website listed by the Muslim Youthwork Foundation.[26]

Now, while such works contain much that is edifying and admirable, some of their material on women, religious pluralism and jihad – as well as the mind-set presupposed by such texts – poses problems in a world very different from the medieval empires in which they were produced.[27] Traditional scholars, thus far, have been ill equipped to engage with such questions other than by curt dismissal. They are unlikely to direct young people to Islamic scholarship produced in academia which addresses such material (assuming they are aware of its existence) – for example, Asma Barlas's research, which traces how women were 'excluded from public life and from the processes of knowledge construction for the thousand or so years that the Muslim empire endured', and which develops a methodology to retrieve the Qur'an's egalitarian potential, buried under the weight of an exegesis that became 'progressively more misogynistic'.[28]

Training *'ulama* in Britain

Most of the traditional schools of Sunni Islam in South Asia have established *madrasa* in Britain.[29] The most successful of these schools has been the Deobandi, whose first *madrasa* was established in 1975 at Bury; the network now consists of 18 such institutions. If the Deobandis in Pakistan could spawn the Taliban – intolerant of other Muslims, not to speak of non-Muslims – the Indian tradition was more eirenic and endorsed the notion of a 'composite nationalism' whereby India could encompass different religious communities. Many Indian Deobandis adopted the politically quietist position of their revivalist wing, Tablighi Jamaat, the preaching party.[30] The latter remain significant in Britain given the dominance of Indian Muslims. However, the Taliban tradition has its apologists amongst British Pakistani Deobandis. The Barelwis, the largest group in Britain, have been much less preoccupied with establishing *madrasa*

– understandable, given the centrality of the Sufi in this tradition. However, they have created five *madrasa*, of which two in particular have developed a good reputation – Eaton Hall, near Nottingham, and Hijaz College in Nuneaton.

Until very recently, students who attended the Deobandi seminaries were socialized in a relatively self-contained world. Islamic study dominated the morning sessions, taught through the medium of Urdu, while a minimal English curriculum was taught in the afternoon to enable pupils from 12 to 16 to conform to the dictates of English law. Students who completed the entire programme of study often lacked good English and the interpersonal skills to relate to wider society. The structure of study guaranteed that students lived in two unconnected intellectual, linguistic and cultural worlds.

The Bury curriculum – *dar-i nizami* – is a reductionist adaptation of one initially developed in eighteenth-century India by the famous Lucknow dynasty of scholars known as the Farangi Mahall. A historian of the movement describes the Farangi Mahall scholars as 'the great consolidators on Indian soil of the rationalist tradition of scholarship derived from Iran'.[31] Their syllabus, with enhanced significance given to logic and philosophy alongside the traditional subjects of the Qur'an, *hadith* and *fiqh* (Islamic jurisprudence), was congenial to the Muslim elites who would become the lawyers, judges and administrators of the Mughal Empire:

> *The study of advanced books of logic, philosophy and dialectic sharpened the rational faculties and . . . brought to the business of government men with better trained minds and better formed judgement . . . the emphasis on the development of reasoning skills meant an emphasis on the understanding rather than merely rote learning . . . It could help . . . to develop opposition to dogmatic and extreme religion . . . [and] bring the continued possibility of a truly understanding interaction with other traditions . . . whether Shia or Hindu.*[32]

Farangi Mahall offered an expansive and innovative curriculum: one of its great nineteenth-century luminaries, Maulana 'Abd al-Hayy, was unusual in embodying in his scholarship a highly developed historical sense. He sought to contextualize the classical texts studied in the seminaries, especially the great works of *fiqh*:

> *He was deeply concerned that the lack of such a sense [of history] amongst his contemporaries meant that they were using all the*

> *elements of the Islamic tradition ... in a wooden and inflexible fashion which made them increasingly less serviceable guides to Islamic behaviour in the present. 'On account of this state of things', he declared somewhat waspishly, 'our ulama have become riders of a blind animal' and fell into a dry well.*[33]

However, with the emergence of the Deobandi tradition in South Asia in the nineteenth century, this tradition of rational sciences and emerging historical contextualization of classical Islamic texts was largely eroded in favour of a renewed emphasis on the revealed sciences of Qur'an and *hadith* and the production of legal verdicts focused upon the moral reform of the individual. There were various reasons for this development, not least the disappearance of the old centres of patronage and demand for the Farangi Mahall education with the collapse of the Mughal Empire and the reduction of Islamic law to personal law. Western education was now the route to positions in British India, which left the *'ulama*, the erstwhile educators of the ruling elite, with the task of the preservation of the core Islamic sciences in what was viewed as a hostile environment.

Bury similarly ignores rational sciences and the contextualization of classical Islamic texts in favour of a renewed emphasis on the revealed sciences of Qur'an and *hadith*.[34] Apart from intense study of Arabic literature and language – the precondition for any serious study of the key Islamic texts – there is some study of the life of the Prophet and his companions and an elementary review of early Islamic history, along with a minimalist selection of medieval texts: a short Qur'anic commentary by Suyuti (d. 1505); a brief text on the articles of belief by Nasafi (d. 1143); and a Hanafi *fiqh* text written by Marghinani (d. 1196), the *Hidaya* mentioned earlier. The apex of study remains the canonical collections of Prophetic traditions (*ahadith*).

Teaching methods aim to initiate the student into the accumulated wisdom of a religious tradition, personalized in the life and teaching of a respected teacher. Teaching is one-way and text-based. The aim is the mastery of key texts and their traditional interpretation rather than the systematic and critical exploration of subjects; successful completion of the course entails the permission (*ijaza*) to teach these texts to a new generation. It is difficult to see how such religious formation can foster a critical traditionalism in dialogue with the complexity of the modern world. An elementary text on Qur'anic exegesis for 12-year-olds used in some Deobandi mosques begins with a health warning to students. It lists the many criteria a scholar has to meet before being considered competent to comment on the Qur'an and concludes with a Prophetic tradition which solemnly warns students against entertaining their own opinion about Qur'anic meanings. They are to depend on the tradition of scholarly mediation. The abode of those who ignore this warning is the 'fire' (of hell).[35]

In the last decade, Bury has made internal changes and furthered its links with external educational institutions, following the lead of graduates who have gained expertise in the wider world. Talk radio is now allowed on campus as well as some broadsheets and weeklies. Many students are opened up to wider currents in Islamic thought through specialist study elsewhere: comparative jurisprudence and Arabic at the Azhar in Egypt, *hadith* studies at the Islamic University of Medina in Saudi Arabia, and training as jurisconsults (*mufti*s) in the Hanafi legal school under such luminaries as the aforementioned Maulana 'Uthmani in Karachi. In the 1990s the abler students were encouraged to get further qualifications from British universities.

The minimal attention given to the English curriculum is also changing. A local college is providing science and computing facilities on site and also personnel to teach examination subjects, both GCSE and A level. I was told on a recent visit in 2007 that they now offer five A levels: in Arabic, Urdu, ICT, Law and Accountancy. Bury has also begun to open up a little to the outside world, especially since 9/11, on the anniversary of which the principal invited a local bishop, a local MP and a few others to visit and talk to students. The principal has also supported a new national Christian–Muslim Forum, initiated in January 2006 with an alumnus chosen as one of its four presidents.[36]

In marked contrast to the Deobandi tradition, it is worth glancing at the ethos and curriculum of the Muslim College in London, which enjoys an influential political role because of the national profile of its founder, the late Sheikh Dr Zaki Badawi. Dr Badawi, an Egyptian scholar trained at Azhar, was one of the few Islamic scholars in Britain at home in both Islamic and modern Western disciplines. He studied psychology at London University and was awarded a Ph.D. on the topic of Islamic modernism. After a stint as Director and Chief Imam at the Islamic Cultural Centre in London, he set up the Muslim College in the mid-1980s to train Muslim scholars.

The Muslim College is a graduate college and in collaboration with Birkbeck College, University of London offers certificate and diploma courses on Islam. It also teaches M.A. students, the first batch qualifying in 1990. To visit the Muslim College website is to enter a world very different from that of the traditional 'seminary'.[37] In the College introduction, there is an acknowledgement that living in a Western environment poses 'a challenge to the ethical and social values enshrined in the Holy Quran and the Sunna'. To meet such challenges, there is 'an imperative to understand Islamic traditional culture in its historical and social context ... a prerequisite for the revitalising of Islamic thought and making Islamic contributions to the realm of ideas relevant to the human condition'.

The College aspires to academic standards comparable to those of other UK institutions of higher education. Unusually for an Islamic institution, the college invites rabbis and clergy to talk to students directly about their different faiths. Students are expected 'to develop a critical approach to traditional and contemporary issues of religion ... to combine theoretical, vocational and practical experiences ... undertake independent research by dealing with both primary and secondary sources ... [and] develop a sense of responsibility towards their community and the welfare of society at large'.

The course offered for imams includes public speaking, with a section on 'psychology of the crowd'; counselling, incorporating 'principles of conciliation'; mosque administration; and a detailed section on understanding the community, which includes work with women, young people, and public bodies such as the police, health authorities, educational institutions and social services. There is also a module on religious dialogue and relations with other religions. Simply to juxtapose the Muslim College's curriculum and ethos to that of a Deobandi *madrasa* is to realize the nature of the challenge facing the latter if they are to equip its English-educated scholars with the intellectual tools to relate confidently to the intellectual, social and cultural world of young British Muslims – especially since the Deobandis, unlike the Barelwi/Sufi tradition, consider music prohibited by Islamic law.

Changing social roles of religious leaders?

The majority of the mosque imams across the country have little or no public and civic role. This is often not understood by policy-makers, who probably operate unconsciously with a mainstream Christian template and assume the imam has a similar civic role to the vicar, or indeed, the Catholic priest or Methodist minister.

The employer of the imam, the mosque committee members, often import an understanding of his roles from back home. Writing of the biggest mosque in a typical Punjabi village, which can accommodate up to between 500 and 600 people for Eid prayers, an anthropologist noted that those who fund and control the mosque

> *do not ask the maulvi to intervene in their disputes and they would not approve if he were to introduce party politics in his sermons. The maulvi's job is to say the* azan, *call to prayers, pray, be moral and rest unobtrusive.*[38]

Some years ago a Deobandi imam in Britain could characterize his functions in the mosque thus:

> *To lead the five daily prayers; to teach the children in the supplementary school; to give the Friday address,* khutbah *(in Arabic) and the accompanying sermon in Urdu; to preside over rites of passage – at birth to whisper the call to prayer,* azaan, *into the child's ear, to solemnize the marriage contract,* nikah, *and to prepare the dead for burial; to prepare* ta'wiz, *amulets, for those fearful of the evil eye; to offer advice, within his competence, on the application of Islamic teaching and law, on a range of issues put to him.*[39]

This minimalist role for the imam is beginning to change for a few pioneers who have moved outside their comfort zones in an attempt to connect with young British Muslims. To illustrate their work I have chosen three *'ulama* known to me personally.

Dr Musharaf Hussain, in his early forties and of Pakistani ancestry, is the founder and inspiration behind the Karimia Institute in Nottingham, which he established in 1990. Dr Hussain has traversed three distinct intellectual and cultural worlds. He acquired his elementary religious education from a Pakistani imam in Bradford, then went on to earn a Ph.D. in medical biochemistry. After some years as a research scholar at a British university he spent a year in a traditional Islamic 'seminary' in Pakistan. He rounded off his Islamic formation by gaining a B.A. in Islamic Studies from Azhar in Cairo. For a while he taught at Jamia Al-Karam, Eaton Hall, Nottingham,.

Karimia Institute is an innovative multi-purpose centre serving the local community. It encloses a mosque, a new sports centre, an accredited nursery, an ITC suite and a number of classrooms and a radio station. Its private primary school is located nearby. Dr Hussain also established a monthly magazine – *The Invitation* – which has been running for more than ten years and now has some 2,000 subscribers and a website. The institute's most recent annual report listed 17 projects, 20 full-time and 35 part-time staff and an annual budget of some £400,000. What is striking in the report has been the emphasis on providing youth with a sense of direction. The institute's staff are involved in a range of partnerships, whether with the local education authority, urban regeneration schemes, local further education college, or youth service. Their work in providing tutorial classes in English, maths and science for the under-16s, as well as offering GCSE in Islamic Studies in Urdu, homework clubs, adult classes and youth provision, all point to their success in such partnerships.

In conversation, Dr Hussain told me that as he engaged with wider society and its agencies his fears and stereotypes began to be challenged. He judges that most local Muslim institutions in the UK are still at the first two stages of creation and consolidation. Few have moved into the critical third phase – 'professionalism'. He is also a founder of a local Muslim charity – Muslim Hands – which now has 16 paid workers and operates in 35 countries with a turnover of several million pounds. Muslim Hands is a professional organization par excellence, winning an 'Investing in People' award: most of the staff have gone through his mosque, local schooling and university.

He has developed many of his initiatives gradually. For seven years the institute ran extra tutorial classes in a variety of subjects. This enabled them to develop a pool of young trained teachers, some of whom now work in their private school. Similarly, they have been licensed by the radio authority to run a local radio station during the month of Ramadan every year since 1996. They have trained a number of people during this time, three of whom have gone on to be journalists with the BBC in various capacities. This gave the Institute the confidence to apply for one of 16 licences given by the Radio Authority across the country for community radio. They were awarded one in 2002, partly because of their willingness to share it with an Asian women's group.

The ethos and concerns of Dr Hussain can be seen in his professionally produced monthly magazine, *The Invitation*. He writes the editorial, one of his Friday sermons becomes the article on the Qur'an, his book of *hadith* translations furnishes a monthly *hadith* reflection, while he acts as resident mufti answering a selection of questions requiring an answer in conformity to Islamic law. His contributions express a broad humaneness, characteristic of the famous Sufi writers he often cites. This is not to accuse his magazine of otherworldliness. He told me that often his editorial is a response to an article in *Newsweek*; he reads eclectically and draws from the Islamist journal, *Impact International*, as well as the English-language monthly *Q-News*. There are articles on fair trade and health matters, as well as articles by local Muslim women. Their self-critical tone is evident in a hard-hitting piece entitled 'Why We Are Where We Are', which includes the following remarks:

> *[Our] dominant chauvinism has trampled upon [women's] God given rights ... Women have become subservient to ... husbands ... extra decoration pieces in their homes ... There are few independent and progressive thinkers in contrast to the vast majority of traditionalists and ritualistic [scholars] ... because it is an easier option as compared to requiring ijtihad or adaptation to the new realities of the modern world. In the absence of any clear vision, today the Muslims present themselves as victims around the world ... [We retreat into] escapism from reality ... [and] we blame the Jews for [all] our ills ... [We need to] build bridges of understanding with the West[.]*[40]

Dr Hussain is one of only two scholars in the Barelwi/Sufi tradition who sit on the central committee of the national Muslim Council of Britain (MCB). Since 9/11 he has been concerned to increase the range of contacts in his local community – not least a joint project with a local church – so as to challenge negative depictions of Muslims. He assumed national media prominence when in September 2004 he and the Assistant Secretary General of the MCB, Dr Daud Abdullah, went off to Iraq, supported by the British Foreign and Commonwealth Office, to intercede for the life of Ken Bigley, a British hostage, later murdered. Dr Hussain had earlier held a much-publicized prayer vigil for Mr Bigley in his local Muslim primary school. Their intervention won much praise for them personally and for the MCB from the British media. The choice of a member of the Muslim Brotherhood and a Sufi to travel together showed a good deal of wisdom, as each could appeal to different constituencies in Iraq.

Dr Hussain is aware that if more *'ulama* are to have the skills and confidence to benefit from the new openness of the local state and public bodies to Islam, there will have to be major changes in religious formation. He sets great store by the Muslim schools movement. There are now over 110 full-time private Muslim schools in the UK, most of which are affiliated to the Association of Muslim Schools

(AMS), set up in 1993, to which he belongs and which he used to chair. He considers that such a network will render many of the Islamic 'seminaries' in Britain irrelevant in the not-too-distant future. The AMS network follows the national curriculum and so Islam is no longer being taught 'out of context' – unlike many Islamic seminaries in the UK, whose medium of instruction remains Urdu and whose curriculum still gives the appearance of being frozen in nineteenth-century India. He surmises that the Muslims will follow the Catholic route and develop a teacher training college within the next decade. Such an institution could draw on the products of the AMS and both offer degrees and pioneer an appropriate Islamic curriculum to develop a new religious leadership at ease in Britain. Such a curriculum could include history, philosophy and the social sciences.

Khalil Ahmed Kazi, a Gujarati in his early thirties, was one of the first Deobandi imams appointed to prison chaplaincy work in 1996 after completing his six-year *'alim* course at Bury. He initially assumed that his role would simply be an extension of his preaching and teaching role in the mosque, which he continues part-time. He discovered that his *'alim* course had furnished him with few transferable work or social skills: he had to master the art of writing complex letters on behalf of inmates to probation officers and review boards; to organize religious festivals in the prison; to develop administrative and managerial skills to equip him to work within a complex hierarchical institution; to acquire the knowledge and confidence to relate to Christian colleagues; to perform a pastoral role for disorientated Muslim prisoners and intercede with fathers whose first response was often to wash their hands of their sons who had brought shame on the extended family; and to build a network of support within the Muslim community for those released. As a chaplain he had a generic role and therefore wider responsibility for all prisoners. Initially, his role as a prison chaplain was met with incredulity within the Muslim community, which was initially in denial about the soaring numbers of Muslim prisoners.

The lessons he has learned as a prison chaplain were applied in Batley, West Yorkshire, where for a couple of years he was General Secretary of an Institute of Islamic Scholars which links some one hundred Deobandi *'ulama*. His first biennial report, for 2000–2, made clear the need both for 'professionalism' in the organization and for increased interaction with wider society. The report was marked by a refreshing candour. Typical was the comment in the Foreword by the chairman, who pointed to the need for

> *True Islamic knowledge and wisdom [in a period] of turmoil and fitnah [chaos]. Each day brings greater challenges and requires insight into complex issues. Many a time it becomes extremely difficult to differentiate between haq [truth] and batil [falsehood] and thus a dilemma is created as to which route one should adopt.*[41]

The organization is between Dr Hussain's second and third phases, consolidation and professionalism. This is clear from Kazi's overview as General Secretary of the institute, where he recounted the shift from ad hoc responses to developing a formal constitution and the introduction of the apparatus of any 'professional' organization – agendas, attendance registers, minutes and even a website. The report indicated an impressive pattern of engagement with wider society, including a chaplaincy group reporting on work in prisons and hospitals; work with local schools and colleges; a *da'wa* (invitation to Islam) and publications department; lecture and youth programmes; a community services network working with the police, MPs and policy-makers; lectures on Islam delivered in a variety of venues, including an Inter-Faith Council; and a support group for drug and alcohol abusers.

There was also no shortage of self-criticism. In the section on Islamic education the report noted that 'the student, after spending a good part of the day at [state] school, comes exhausted both mentally and physically to the *madrasah*. If the [teacher] then conducts his lesson without any preparation, planning or using relevant methods, how would that capture the imagination, attention and hearts of the students?' One major concern clearly articulated in the report is the limited expectations parents have of Islamic education: 'Their idea of Islamic education is no more than the ability to read the Qur'an … [U]nder the pretext of flimsy excuses, such as increased school workload or attending weddings', they deprive them of basic knowledge of Islam. This creates an identity crisis when they reach adolescence.

As a prison chaplain, Kazi is well aware of the growing disaffection of young Gujarati Muslims from the mosque. In Batley, where he serves as a part-time imam, he has started meetings for these disenchanted young Muslims in a community centre, a neutral space outside the mosque. Able to bridge the worlds of mosque, prison and wider society, he has developed some innovative projects in partnership with local agencies. The one which has given him most satisfaction was launched in Batley in April 2004 at a Muslim community centre – an

Islamic drug awareness service, We Can Kick It, with accompanying website.[42]

This project – which aims to work with the hard-to-reach groups in local mosques, schools and community centres, and involves all fifty of Batley's mosques – has been devised by Khalil, as Muslim consultant and project co-ordinator, with a number of Muslim professionals – two drugs trainers from the health authority, a sports researcher and community liaison officer – who have devised the material to be used in the mosque with 11-year-olds. The material has been tested with schools and the project has been funded by police and drug action teams. Those who complete the two-hour course, whether in mosque, community centre or school, are given a certificate and access to sports training programmes as an alternative to the 'hanging out' and drug misuse culture.

For Khalil the key to the success of such ventures is partnership – partnership between Muslim scholars and Muslim professionals and partnership with a variety of agencies now willing to work with religious groups. The police going into mosques to speak about drugs awareness would have been unheard of a couple of years earlier. The mosques used to be closed worlds, with many of the elders and *'ulama* deeply suspicious of non-Muslim society. Khalil candidly acknowledged to me that the shock of 9/11 has enabled him to open up this closed world – as a respected traditionalist religious scholar himself he has been able to negotiate access to such agencies, legitimize such initiatives Islamically, and provide Islamic support materials.

Khalil and a few like-minded British-educated *'ulama* have developed a new set of social and intellectual skills, working outside a Muslim subculture of 'seminary' and mosque. This indicates a growing awareness of the need to connect with streetwise British Muslim youth and the growing willingness of support agencies to work with them. Ahmed Ali, a Pakistani in his early thirties, serves a largely Pakistani constituency in Bradford. He too has established an independent Islamic institution, staffed and run largely by Bury-educated *'ulama*. Like Dr Hussain, Ahmed enjoys the additional prestige of a B.A. degree in Islamic study at Azhar in Cairo.

The aim of such an independent institution is both freedom from control by mosque committee elders and freedom from the negative associations mosques often have in the minds of Muslim youth. It organizes a range of activities for Muslim youth intended to maintain their interest through adolescence – the major problem Khalil has identified. Ahmed runs additional educational classes at the weekends in computing, English and maths, as well as homework clubs. Everything is studied through the medium of English. He and his colleagues seek to supplement and consolidate state education. In the summer Ahmed takes youngsters camping, and organizes day trips to local theme parks. In co-operation with youth workers they provide soccer at weekends and competitions in the summer. Groups of young men attend the annual Islamic study camp held at Kidderminster, where Ahmed is one of the few non-Gujarati speakers. Ahmed is quite clear that his Islamic Academy is to be understood as a social centre generating a wide range of activities not normally associated with a mosque.

Ahmed has also pioneered an attractively produced series of Islamic storybooks in English for children, each based on an imaginative rewriting of a *hadith*. The first, entitled *The Bully King*, was produced in 2000 and eight others have been printed. However, his particular strength is as a charismatic speaker who has developed an audiotape and CD ministry.[43] He has produced over sixty titles and sells tens of thousands of copies every year, not least in the United States. He does not avoid controversial issues, whether drugs, or forced marriage. A recent tape is amusingly entitled 'The IT Syndrome', where he parodies the 'big-timers' and role models for disaffected youth in the community, with their '7 series BMWs, Mercs and mobile phones' who forget the Qur'an's warnings about 'exalting riches and forgetting Allah'. He reminds them of the Qur'anic punishments – amputation for theft; 'eighty of the best' for false accusation; stoning for adultery with a married woman. He goes into gruesome detail about the humiliations of hell. Ahmed makes no concessions to liberal Western sensibilities.

Two tapes concerning marriage indicate that his rootedness in the Islamic tradition provides a strong platform from which to criticize cultural abuses. Thus he can address the issue of 'Forced Marriage' and acknowledges that it is a widespread abuse in the South Asian communities – 'some are blackmailed, some are threatened, some are severely beaten'. Drawing on Hanafi jurisprudence, he points out that Islamic legal norms insist that the wife is not a commodity – she has rights to a modest dowry and must give her permission to marriage. He reminds the men in his audience that the essential factor in choosing a partner is not wealth, status or beauty but her piety, with marriage understood as a form of worship. He concedes that piety is not the first concern of many parents, who are more preoccupied in marrying off 'this or that uncle/aunt's son or daughter'. Further, a guardian should take account of an Islamic norm – equality of status (*kuf*). He is also deeply critical of conspicuous consumption at weddings – what he amusingly refers to as 'blow [all your savings] and show [off your supposed wealth]' – and the popularity of Hindu customs. Along with much sensible advice, he mentions that if men contemplate multiple wives – no more than four, of course – they must treat them with 'equality and justice'.

He is clearly exercised by the encroachment of non-Muslim cultural practices. In a recent cassette – *Tawheed and Shirk* – he reminds his audience that *shirk*, 'associating' something or someone with Allah, is the unforgivable sin. He expresses dismay that some misguided Muslims protested against the Taliban's destruction of the Buddhist statues in Afghanistan. He recounts with approval a tradition to the effect that a companion of the Prophet was commended for cleaving the head of a female seer. Yet all around him Ahmed sees Muslims adopting unacceptable practices, whether consulting their zodiac signs in the tabloid press or celebrating Valentine's Day. He also repeats an intra-Muslim polemic against practices such as praying at the tombs of Islamic saints for children. All such activities are tantamount to *shirk*, since only Allah has knowledge of the future and of the unseen.

In his two most recent CDs – *Do Not Despair* and *The Future is Bright* – he recounts the humiliations and defeats of the Muslim world during the last fifty years. Kashmir begins the catalogue of horrors – murder, torture and rape of mothers and daughters – with the point that 'the so-called civilized world deliberately turns a blind eye': 'Where else in the world do you see anyone else other than Muslims being persecuted and tortured? ... If one non-Muslim is persecuted all of a sudden there is a huge cry in the name of human rights'. The same pattern is detailed in relation to Palestine, with the same refrain: 'They say we live in a civilized world; yet, such atrocities were not committed in the dark ages.'

He moves on to the post-9/11 situation, where even in Britain Muslims are, he claims, 'interrogated, harassed and humiliated' at airports, singled out and accused of terrorism. 'We have to prove our innocence'. This rendering of recent Muslim history continues with stories of rape, torture and atrocities, with 'millions of Muslims being slaughtered'. The answer to this catalogue of horrors is not to doubt the power of Allah. Rather, all this is to be construed as a test whereby the truth of Muslim commitment is exposed. How else does one prove oneself worthy of *Jannah* (Paradise)?

The positive message is that Muslims should take a lead from a famous incident in the Prophet's life, the Treaty of Hudaibiya, whereby his enemies in Mecca agreed to a truce for ten years, but denied him and his followers access to the city. There was much grumbling among the Prophet's companions at such concessions. This triggered a famous Qur'anic verse which insists that in the long view this truce would be seen as a 'clear [manifest] victory' (48.1). Such it proved. Ahmed reminds his readers that 'the conquests lay hidden in this truce'. After all, the Meccan leaders had dealt with the Prophet as an accredited equal. The burden of endless fighting and anti-Muslim propaganda – likened to the BBC, Channel 4 and ITV today – was lifted; the secret believers in Mecca began to pray openly and non-Muslims were able to interact and hold dialogue with Muslims and be exposed to the beautiful teachings of Islam. So, within two years of the truce 'more embraced Islam than in the previous 16 years'. The *kuffar* (infidels) began to join Islam in huge numbers and victory was assured.

Ahmed points out that the recent international media scrutiny of Islam, whether positive or negative, has done what a 'hundred years of Muslim effort [preaching] could not achieve'. It has been a wake-up call for Muslims across the world, including Muslims in the West. '*They realized that they would never be accepted.* So they are deserting the bars and nightclubs and returning to Islam'.

> *In Britain, too, young Muslims at universities and workplaces who had forgotten their identity ... post-9/11 with [people] looking at them in an evil way and seeing them as terrorists [now realize]* we will never be accepted ... *[so they] return to Islam ... sisters are wearing* hijab ... *the Lion is waking up.*

Ahmed Ali's discourse reflects a number of key themes which are also evident in Riyadhul Haq's talk, to which reference has already been made: the Muslim as victim; a Manichaean discourse pitting Muslim and antagonistic non-Muslim world against each other; and a utopian, even millenarian rhetoric where the *umma* will prevail over its enemies and win a 'clear victory'.

Conclusion: only connect?

Surprisingly, 9/11 and 7/7 have not proved an unmitigated disaster for Muslim communities. Some *'ulama* have seen it as a wake-up call for Muslims to venture out from their comfort zones and relatively closed communities to explain themselves to the media and to engage with professionals in wider society – whether clergy, teachers, social workers or police – to address youth disaffection and contribute to raising worryingly low educational standards amongst a section of Muslim youth.

Many of the English-educated *'ulama* discussed in this chapter are very able and have successfully negotiated multiple worlds. However, even they fall into two categories: some are 'cosmopolitan', others 'transnational'. The latter, in contrast to the former, are 'rarely heard and even more rarely recognised and listened to beyond their own communities. They speak a foreign language or enunciate alien, widely unacceptable sentiments'.[44] It is clear that two of the *'ulama* discussed – Riyadhul Haq and Ahmed Ali – could probably be characterized as transnational in this sense. Both were trained and socialized in a relatively closed Islamic environment without direct exposure – unlike the others – to Western tertiary education or the need to develop new social and intellectual skills as teachers or chaplains – what most refer to, for the sake of brevity, as 'professionalism'.

It is also evident that if more British-educated *'ulama* are to follow these pioneers, certain structural weaknesses in both mosque culture and seminary will have to be addressed. Most of the *'ulama* discussed have felt the need either to set up independent institutions or to maintain their economic independence of mosque committees. However able an imam in a mosque is, he is usually poorly remunerated and lacks contractual security.

Clearly, *madrasa* formation will have to make space to include new skills, intellectual, social and communicational. At the moment, it can take as long as ten years for the most able seminarians to feel at ease in wider society. If these issues are not addressed the danger will be the creation of a two-tier system of *'ulama*: those least able to understand and connect with the concerns of British Muslims will find employment inside the mosque; those most able to connect will have to find employment outside it.

In the long term, there remains an urgent need for the creation of Islamic institutions which combine the best of traditional scholarship with modern disciplines. This was a need identified within Pakistan almost a quarter of a century ago, where it still has not been met.[45] The Muslim College in London remains the best approximation to such an institution in Britain. However, as will be clear from the changes evident in curriculum and ethos at the Bury *madrasa*, it is not impossible that the Deobandi school might also, in time, develop the skills and confidence to include new academic disciplines that better equip their students to understand British culture and history. A necessary but not sufficient change will be the shift from Urdu to English as the medium of instruction.

At the moment, the Islamic Sunni tradition which has most successfully embedded itself institutionally in Britain is that of the Deobandi. However, it is clear that their prohibition on music means they have a mountain to climb if they wish to engage with young Muslims. Also, their conservative attitudes towards gender and gender segregation mean that many of the best-educated women will likely look elsewhere for religious guidance. It remains to be seen whether they can change their pedagogical style to engage with the exploratory identity of many young British Muslims, the desideratum for a robust and confident Muslim personality, as indicated by the Muslim theologian and educationalist Dr Sahin, to whose important research a number of references have already been made.

Dr Mahmood Chandia, after study at Bury and Azhar, went on to complete a Ph.D. in Islamic Studies at Manchester University. His career trajectory indicates that it is possible to encompass insights from all three linguistic and educational worlds. He lectures at a local university, as well as being involved in the Lancashire Council of Mosques. The future of the Deobandi tradition will turn on whether his experience of confident engagement with wider society becomes the norm, or whether the suspicion of Riyadhul Haq will continue to shape its ethos.

Notes

1. This conference took place in 2004. In the following year, the year of 7/7, it was judged probably unwise to hold such a gathering, which would invite the interest of the intelligence services. Sheikh Yusuf Motala had already had a brush with the security services in November 2003 when they detained him en route during pilgrimage.

2. Both appear on the Bury multi-lingual website, <www.inter-Islam.org>.

3. The prophecy of the ultimate triumph of Islam appears three times in the Qur'an: 9.33, 48.28 and 61.9.

4. R. Bulliett, *Islam: The View from the Edge* (New York: Columbia University Press, 1994), p. 187.

5. J. Birt, 'Wahhabism in the United Kingdom: Manifestations and Reactions', in M. Al-Rasheed (ed.), *Transnational Connections and the Arab Gulf* (London: Routledge, 2005), provides a useful entry point into the topic of Wahhabi influence.

6. Z. Badawi, *Islam in Britain* (London: Ta Ha, 1981), p. 23.

7. See A. Caeiro, 'Transnational 'Ulama, European Fatwas, and Islamic Authority: A Case Study of the European Council for Fatwa and Research', in M. van Bruinessen (ed.), *Producing Islamic Knowledge: Transmission and Dissemination in Western Europe* (London: Routledge, 2007).

8. F. Robinson, *Separatism among Indian Muslims: The Politics of the United Provinces' Muslims 1860–1923* (Cambridge: Cambridge University Press, 1974), p. 263, citing an unpublished seminar paper by P. Hardy.

9. See 'Home-Grown Imams to Curb Hate Preachers', *Sunday Times*, 1 April 2007.

10. S. McLoughlin, 'The Mosque-Centre, Community-Mosque: Multi-Functions, Funding and the Reconstruction of Islam in Bradford', *Scottish Journal of Religious Studies*, 19 (1998), pp. 211–27.

11. J. Malik, 'Madrasah in South Asia', in I. Abu-Rabi (ed.), *The Blackwell Companion to Contemporary Islamic Thought* (Oxford: Blackwell Publishing, 2006), p. 113.

12. S. Gilliat-Ray, 'Educating the 'Ulama: Centres of Islamic Religious Training in Britain', *Islam and Christian–Muslim Relations*, 17 (2006), p. 70.

13. S. M. Lyon, *An Anthropological Analysis of Local Politics and Patronage in a Pakistani Village* (Lampeter: Edwin Mellen, 2004), p. 221.

14. See P. Werbner, *Pilgrims of Love: The Anthropology of a Global Sufi Cult* (London: Hurst and Co., 2003).

15. M. Zaman, 'Pluralism, Democracy and the 'Ulama', in R. Heffner (ed.), *Remaking Muslim Politics: Pluralism, Contestation, Democratization* (Princeton: Princeton University Press, 2005), p. 71.

16. See A. H. Nayyar and A. Salim, *The Subtle Subversion: The State of Curricula and Textbooks in Pakistan* (Islamabad: Sustainable Development Policy Institute, 2004).

17. H. Ansari, *The Infidel Within: Muslims in Britain since 1800* (London: Hurst and Co., 2004), p. 346.

18. T. Abbas, *Muslim Britain: Communities Under Pressure* (London: Zed Books, 2005).

19. B. Wazir, 'Mosques: Sources of Comfort, or Out of Touch?', *The Times*, 26 July 2004.

20. Muslim Women's Network and Women's National Commission, *She Who Disputes: Muslim Women Shape the Debate*, p. 52; the text is available at <www.thewnc.org/uk/pubs/shewhodisputesnov06.pdf>. In Bradford, an official of the Bradford Council for Mosques recently told me that he was unaware of any women involved in mosque committees in the city.

21. Ibid., pp. 50, 52, 32.

22. See <www.forum.mpcak.org>, last accessed 2 April 2005. The *Independent* article continues: '[When] … an imam at the Birmingham Central Mosque secretly married a woman who became his second wife … a scandal broke when

... the mosque secretary ... had an affair with the woman and she became pregnant ... [and was] demonised by followers of the imam'.

23. A. S. Ahmed, *Islam Under Siege: Living Dangerously in a Post-Honor World* (Cambridge: Polity Press, 2003), p. 144.

24. Zaman, Pluralism, Democracy and the 'Ulama', p. 68. Pakistan's finest modernist scholar, Fazlur Rahman, also dismissed 'on historical grounds ... [the arguments of] those modern Muslim apologists who have tried to explain the *jihad* of the early Community in purely defensive terms': *Islam* (New York: Anchor Books, 1968), p. 34.

25. P. Lewis, *Islamic Britain: Religion, Politics and Identity among British Muslims* (London: I. B. Tauris, 2002), p. 139.

26. See <www.sunnipath.com> under 'Resources', where the work is listed as *Riyad as Salihin* with translation by Ayesha Bewley. According to a new English translation of the Qur'an, a phrase used to justify 'humiliation' of People of the Book in traditional exegesis (9.29) has been misunderstood and does not carry this negative meaning. See M. A. S. Abdel Haleem, *The Qur'an: A New Translation* (Oxford: Oxford University Press, 2004), p. 118.

27. Other popular works, such as a fourteenth-century manual of Islamic law by Ahmad ibn Naqib al-Misi, *Reliance of the Traveller*, ed. N. H. M. Keller (Beltsville, Md: Amana Publications, 1994 edn), embody similar perspectives.

28. A. Barlas, 'Women's Readings of the Qur'an', in J. D. McAuliffe (ed.), *The Cambridge Companion to the Qur'an* (Cambridge: Cambridge University Press, 2006), p. 257. Barlas's essay is a good point of entry into this emerging field of female Muslim scholarship. A. Sachedina, *The Islamic Roots of Democratic Pluralism* (Oxford: Oxford University Press, 2001), also traces how the 'pluralistic spirit' of the Qur'an was replaced by 'Muslim jurists who encouraged a state-sponsored institutionalisation of the inferiority of non-Muslims ... [considered to have] wilfully spurned the offer of Islam ... [It was] this kind of evaluation of the religious other that led to the contemptuous attitude toward non-Muslim minorities in Muslim societies' (p. 97).

29. See J. Birt and P. Lewis, 'The Pattern of Islamic Reform in Britain: The Deobandis between Intra-Muslim Sectarianism and Engagement with Wider Society', in M. van Bruinessen (ed.), *Producing Islamic Knowledge: Transmission and Dissemination in Western Europe* (London: Routledge, 2007).

30. See Y. Sikand, *The Origin and Development of the Tablighi Jama'at (1920–2000)* (New Delhi: Longman, 2002).

31. F. Robinson, *The Ulama of Farangi Mahall and Islamic Culture in South Asia* (Delhi: Orient Longman, 2001), p. 2.

32. Ibid., pp. 53–4.

33. Ibid., p. 121.

34. The curriculum of Deobandi and Barelwi 'seminaries' is similar. The main contrast is that Barelwis teach in English and give more importance to the English curriculum for youngsters from 13 to 16. Their ethos is also more relaxed and 'open' to wider society. See S. Gilliat-Ray, 'Closed Worlds: (Not) Accessing Deobandi dar ul-uloom in Britain', *Fieldwork in Religion*, 1 (2005), pp. 7–33.

35. *Tasheel Durusil Quraan: Lessons of the Quraan Made Easy*, vol. 8 (Lenasia, South Africa: The Syllabi Committee,

Jamiyatul Ulama Taalimi Board, n.d.), p. 5.

36. For details of Sheikh Yusuf Motala's statement in support of the Christian–Muslim Forum, delivered at the northern conference held on 15 November 2006, see <www.christianmuslimforum.org>, 'Northern reception'.

37. See <www.muslimcollege.ac.uk>.

38. Lyon, *An Anthropological Analysis*, p. 218.

39. Lewis, *Islamic Britain*, p. 117.

40. F. R. Khan, 'Why We Are Where We Are', *Invitation*, September 2002, pp. 24–5.

41. I am grateful to Khalil for furnishing me with the document (undated and unpaginated).

42. See <www.wecankickit.co.uk>.

43. Quotations and paraphrases from his speeches are based on my own transcriptions of the tapes and CDs, none of which are dated.

44. P. Werbner, *Imagined Diasporas among Manchester Muslims* (Oxford: James Curry, 2002), pp. 6–7.

45. F. Rahman, *Islam and Modernity: Transformation of an Intellectual Tradition* (Chicago: University of Chicago Press, 1982), pp. 110-25.

CHAPTER 5

British Muslims, Radical Islam and its Critics

A useful window into the recruitment techniques, appeal and ideology of radical Islam in Britain is provided in an account by an ex-member of Hizb ut-Tahrir (HT) – the Palestinian Islamist movement which broke away from the Muslim Brotherhood in the 1950s. Shiraz Maher, who used to be its Leeds regional organizer, begins his story of his own recruitment with a question put to him by the person who would become his mentor:

> *'So, brother, what do you think of 9/11?' . . . It's just days after the terrorist atrocity and I'm sipping mint tea in his living room. 'Of course, America will use this to wage war on Islam,' he tells me. I wasn't immediately convinced, but was certainly willing to hear more. That was the problem.*
>
> *Wherever I went, everyone was talking about 9/11. Everyone, that is, except those at the mosques I was attending – they simply buried their heads in the sand. I found it frustrating at the time, but . . . [their silence allowed] extremist groups such as the one I joined, Hizb at-Tahrir (HT), to seize their opportunity.*
>
> *After my initial contact with the party, we met quite intensively and I was told I had a duty to 'defend Islam' from the impending 'humiliation' America was about to inflict. I was told the single most important issue facing the Muslim world was the revival of the caliphate, a theocratic pan-Islamic state uniting all the Muslim lands under a single leader.*
>
> *It seems absurd now, but at the time it made perfect sense: the party would inspire a revolution 'somewhere' in the Muslim world; a caliphate would be declared, and it would then conquer the world. As*

> *a student, I was on the front line. I soon realised just how important universities were for Islamist groups: for young people eager for new ideas they provided an environment far removed from the deadening conservatism of the mosques.*

Shiraz explains that HT also considered the mosque a good place for recruitment, whether inside the building or leafleting outside. Since with 85 per cent of imams having come from outside Britain, they are 'impotent' – 'unable to give any meaningful direction to young British Muslims, having never experienced the kinds of problems or challenges that they face'.

This is where radical movements – such as HT and its recently banned splinter movement, al Muhajirun – come into their own. They are composed overwhelmingly of young men, just like their target audience. Schooled in the language of modernity and versed in the idioms of Britain's liberal democracy, they are adept at presenting their message.

Speaking of his recruitment, Shiraz admits:

> *I wasn't too concerned with religious practice, I wouldn't go to the mosque all too often but I'd tick the box which said 'Muslim' when filling out the census forms. My contact with HT was at the local mosque where I met a young man who had just graduated with a degree from Durham University in Arabic and politics. I was struck by the fact that he was an intellectual and had obviously worked hard to better himself and win a place at university . . . he was also a hafiz . . . someone who memorises the entire Qur'an by heart. So here was someone who was really moving forward both temporally and spiritually despite having come from a deprived background. He didn't look like the typical 'mad mullah' – and wore normal clothes and sported only a short, trimmed beard.*
>
> *The core HT idea is 'to live with the ummah'. The idea is that you live within a [Muslim] community and must therefore not just be part of it –* but must seek to lead it. *You must feel its local problems, sense its local realities and seek to capitalise on this by* superimposing an Islamist template*[.]*

As well as recruiting at university, they seek to embody a model community. Hizb ut-Tahrir consider that they have reached a critical mass in terms of membership, with a large and established infrastructure across the country. Now they are seeking to gain intellectual and political leadership and serve as a vanguard for their interests. Thus they aim to capitalize on populist issues, e.g. the controversy surrounding the Danish cartoons. Hizb ut-Tahrir sought to exploit Muslim anger on this issue by organizing several demonstrations which were responsibly conducted but nonetheless skewed towards the party's objectives. By contrast, this template can work on the micro-level too. Members of HT were at the forefront of a campaign in Stoke-on-Trent a few years ago to oppose the opening of a pornography shop in their local community. It was a great coup for the party, which allowed them to take leadership of the community while driving their agenda forward.

In recent years, much of their radical, anti-Western rhetoric has been toned down and they have sought to portray themselves as family-friendly. This has prompted the launching of publications like *Salam Magazine*, which is marketed as a 'Muslim Lifestyle Magazine' covering such topics as money, saving tips and educational advice for Muslim parents. But behind this 'glossy façade', Shiraz insists, its objectives remain the same:

- Win new recruits.
- Assume leadership of the wider Muslim community.
- Alienate Muslims from the non-Muslim community, to prevent the two from integrating, thereby promoting an agenda of self-reliance – with participation in democratic politics dismissed as *kufr* [un-belief].
- Work to undermine existing [Muslim] regimes and re-establish the caliphate – abolished by Ataturk in 1924.

Britain remains for HT the front line in their global Islamist network, especially London, with its formidable infrastructure of financial, logistical and intellectual capital. Pakistan, in particular, is a key target for HT – and an area where it is actively seeking to establish a caliphate. That nation is also a nuclear power. Pakistan's *Asia Times* commented in June 2005:

> *Hundreds of HT members, British but of Pakistani origin, many of them students at the London School of Economics, and other centres of excellence, packed their bags and departed for Pakistan. By 2000, HT established itself in all urban centres of the country.*

While conducting a campaign against President Musharraf of Pakistan in 2003, HT urged mosque-goers to 'realise your international influence and stop Busharraf'. This leaflet, distributed nationwide after Friday prayers, said, 'the time has come for Muslims in Britain to impact upon the work to re-establish the *Khilafah* [caliphate] in the Muslim world. This is only the beginning; soon Muslims in the West will send delegations to the Muslim world calling upon our people to rise to the challenge and fulfil the promise of Allah.' It concluded: 'Oh Muslims in Britain! Our place in history awaits us – if only we seize our opportunity . . . we call upon you to fulfil your global role.'

Shiraz seeks to explain the attraction of movements such as HT, in part, as a reaction to

> *the* Biradari *system – an unwritten code of social honour which subjugates the individual to the community and is a system perpetuated by the 'elders'. It necessarily disenfranchises the young.*
>
> *By contrast Islamist groups empower the youth – and not just men, but women too. This is radical. They encourage women to participate in public life, to pursue an education, to oppose arranged marriages and to engage in political activism – most of which is still very uncommon among Islamist groups. This . . . makes these groups seem progressive.*[1]

Fatima Khan, a young East Ender from a Pakistani background, also joined HT. Her story supports Shiraz's analysis. In the context of a traditional Punjabi community, at once 'pious and patriarchal', Fatima was aware that it was considered shameful to emulate the customs and manners of the English. Yet, when she began to work in Oxford Street she found herself free to meet other people and found it liberating. At home, she could never be herself. At a time of personal crisis, a radical Islamic identity became an attractive alternative which seemed to transcend regional cultures and at the same time to offer a clear, powerful and universal message.

Fatima separated from her husband, and her family, unable to face the shame, disowned her. At 22 she found herself on her own with four children in a cockroach-infested flat in the East End. The radical group she joined accepted her, at a time when she needed acceptance. She was impressed by one particular speaker because he was talking about global issues – Palestine and Bosnia:

> *Suddenly we were part of a bigger thing – this global family we had. Not only was I accepted, I was suddenly exclusive . . . because I am a Muslim . . . I'm part of something bigger, greater and we're going*

> *to go to heaven. We thought everyone else had got it wrong. We were not sitting around plotting and planning how to blow up this or that but [thought that] if we get empowerment eventually we will be strong enough to overthrow these ['Muslim'] governments ... Our struggle in the West was one of ideology ... about changing the way you were thinking ... about educating people into why we had to change the world.*[2]

Political Islam – Islamism – has two interconnected aims, both about reviving Muslim identity. In Muslim countries, this can mean creating perfect Islamic states, either through persuasion or violence. Where Muslims are in a minority, such as Britain, Islamism is more about solidarity with the *umma*, the global Muslim community. Aminul Hoque, a 28-year-old journalist and Ph.D., student, has seen HT's recruiting methods at close quarters in his East London Bangladeshi community:

> *Once young people, in particular ... leave the doors of the mosque, they are entering the political sphere. And you can literally see ... on the mosque doorstep people who are angry, who are politicized, giving out leaflets and [declaring] what is happening in Afghanistan is wrong, look at what they're doing in Iraq, how many people are dying as a consequence. This was about oil and never about human rights or democracy. And those people who have become conscious and aware of themselves as Muslims first and foremost in the mosque have come out all peace, all calm, and suddenly they've become angry because they've got this feeling of attack, that everyone's against us*[.][3]

From radical rhetoric to radical politics

Hizb ut-Tahrir is but one more expression of radicalism which has agitated Britain's Muslim communities for more than twenty years. This party can be positioned at the confluence of at least three streams of experience. First, there is 'an oppositional postcolonial sensibility' which generates 'a suspicion in principle of the publicly declared good intentions of successive British governments'.[4] This is particularly evident in Pakistan and amongst Pakistani diasporas. A comparative sociological study completed before 9/11 of four Muslim majority countries, one of which was Pakistan, revealed 'how Muslims see an increasing moral polarization between themselves and the "Other" globally ... [which] does not augur well for promoting better political relationships between Western countries and the Muslim world'.[5] In the Pakistani sample 79 per cent considered the UK government anti-Islamic.[6] The UK was seen as pro-India and culpable in not using its influence to defend Bosnia.

Secondly, there is an ever-expanding list of British Muslim grievances, whether on British foreign policy, social and economic exclusion, or Islamophobia in the media and wider society which disparages and demeans Islam – grievances which, of course, intensify after 9/11 with draconian anti-terrorist legislation, perceived as having a disproportionate impact on Muslim communities. This can soon translate into a debilitating sense of victimhood. Thirdly, many Muslims imagine their collective social life – what social scientists refer to as the 'social imaginary' – within a utopian and millenarian framework. In short, 'the postcolonial sensibility meshes with the Islamic utopianist one to create a political perspective suspicious of the good intentions of the West in general', not to speak of Britain in particular.[7]

The first two factors are well researched, the third less so. Millenarian views are frequently found at times of rapid social change and uncertainty, and often with people who find themselves on the periphery of political and cultural influence. Muslims can also appeal to aspects of the Islamic eschatology embedded in the textual tradition. For most of Islamic history, these notes are muted. However, at times of perplexity and collective failure they reappear.

These three factors were already at play in the early 1990s. In October 1990 Pakistani Muslims from the majority Barelwi/Sufi traditionalist school of thought met at Manchester Town Hall to celebrate the Birthday of the Prophet. An anthropologist who heard the accompanying speeches was surprised to discover that on the eve of the first Gulf war, Saddam Hussein was firmly established as a public hero. There was little sympathy for Kuwaitis. Talk of violations of international law and defying the UN charter was met with cynicism and counter-questions: What about Kashmir? And Palestine? Where has UN justice been in relation to these countries? She concluded that British Pakistanis seemed to be setting themselves morally apart from British society:

> *They expressed no horror at Saddam Hussein's tyranny and no sorrow or concern for 'our boys', at risk in the Gulf. Instead, they spoke of Christian soldiers desecrating the holy ground of the Hijaz [in Saudi Arabia], of Western aggression, of a Western medieval Crusader revival, of the need for jihad. Thus they placed themselves*

> *almost entirely outside the broad moral consensus which encompassed both war and peace movements.*[8]

The West and its media were frequently demonized. British media coverage was dismissed by one speaker as providing only the 'most poisonous, most biased and most prejudiced information'. The media was seen as presenting distorted images of the Islamic world, lies and propaganda, concocted for a Western audience. 'This complete lack of trust in the veracity and independence of the media means that even the most public "facts", such as the plight of the Kurdish refugees, are taken by Pakistanis to represent something other than their obvious meaning for a Western audience.' The speeches also embodied an almost millennial faith that God would protect his followers from diabolical conspiracies, as in this excerpt:

> *So God is God, man proposes, God disposes, and in this case I think Bush proposes and God disposes [of him]. These people [Bush and the Western powers] are in for a big shock, those who are thinking that they will control the destiny of the Gulf. They look upon the [crisis] as an Arab question, an oil question, a Middle Eastern question – I say to them: No! This is a Muslim question [so God will dispose it.]*[9]

Such populist Islamic radicalism, generated by Sufi, imam and lay preacher, was, in reality, confined to rhetoric, and was soon disappointed: 'The swings between temporary utopian hopes for Islamic dominance and a sense of communal failure and total powerlessness were more evident in their speeches than any determination to engage in sustained practical political action'.[10] This episode encapsulates a number of themes which have undergone a double expansion since, in extension and intensity: deep mistrust of Western media; a loss of confidence in the UN and other international bodies because of their failures or double standards in Israel/Palestine, Iraq, Bosnia and Kashmir; and a readiness to support periodic utopian projects.

Radicalism was given a new lease of life with Ayatollah Khomeini and the Iranian revolution. Among its acolytes was the late Kalim Siddiqui (d. 1996), ex-*Guardian* journalist, whose intellectual wanderings from Marxist sympathies and Trotskyite leanings, via Saudi support for his think-tank, the Muslim Institute in London, to apologist for every aspect of the Iranian revolution, have been amusingly documented by a fellow-traveller, Ziauddin Sardar, who unlike Siddiqui soon became disillusioned with apologist and revolution alike.[11] However, Siddiqui was able to capitalize on Muslim anger generated by the Rushdie affair, especially among the new generation of British-educated Muslims, for whom the affair was their first experience of political activity.

It is hard now to capture the excitement and hopes which the Iranian revolution generated among Islamists attracted to Kalim Siddiqui's Muslim Institute. One such activist was Dr Ghayasuddin Siddiqui, who had been, with Ziauddin Sardar, a member of the Federation of Student Islamic Societies in UK and Eire (FOSIS), which in 1970 already had a significant institutional presence as a bearer of political Islam, imported from Pakistan with Jama'at-i Islami (JI) or Egypt with the Muslim Brotherhood (MB), Islamist movements set up in the 1920s and 1930s.[12]

Ghayasuddin's parents, like many Indian Muslims, had migrated to Pakistan in 1947, where he became a leader in the student wing of JI and an ardent admirer of its founder, Abu Ala Mawdudi (d. 1979). For Mawdudi, Islam was a revolutionary ideology that sought to alter the social order of the entire world. However, unlike extremist elements of the MB – supporters of the influential views of Sayyid Qutb, brutalized and executed in one of Nasser's prisons in 1966 – JI never supported violent revolution. Ghayasuddin continued his activities in England, where he gained a doctorate in production engineering at Sheffield University.

In a recent interview, he makes clear why a Shia revolution in 1979 was so important to Sunni Islamists like him. Until 1979 political Islam in either its MB or JI form had been little more than a dream, with little possibility of capturing power. Now it had become a reality, with Muslim scholars toppling one of the most oppressive regimes in the Middle East, supported by the United States:

> *In Iran revolutionary guards play a very, very significant role. And many of the [future] revolutionary guards were students in Britain, so as such were our close friends, so whenever we went to Iran, we were obviously their guests and they would look after us ... I remember one day that we wanted to go somewhere and we were getting late ... [a revolutionary guard] said, 'No, no, no, that is no problem' and we took a helicopter ... this left a great impression. And immediately I realized that I know it really is true that if an ideology can control state resources, then it can do whatever it wants.*[13]

Such enthusiasms lay behind the creation of Kalim Siddiqui's radical but ill-starred 'Muslim Parliament', launched in a blaze of publicity in January 1992. His inaugural address embodied his own variant of political millenarianism. He lambasted Western civilization as

> *the modern world's sick man ... destined for oblivion ... [with Islam] the antidote to a morally bankrupt world ... [the] Muslim Parliament [embodies the] Prophetic example [of] how to generate the political power of Islam in a minority situation and how to nurse [it] ... until the creation of an Islamic state and the victory of Islam over all its opponents.*[14]

Such heady rhetoric attracted many idealistic young Muslim professionals, hand-picked by Siddiqui as members of his parliament. The Muslim Parliament, after Siddiqui's death in 1996, led at best an attenuated existence following a number of splits. Dr Ghayasuddin, who led it for a while, has increasingly distanced himself from political Islam.[15]

In the early 1990s mainstream Islamist groups were continuing to debate the comparative merits of engagement versus resistance. In August 1991 the UK Islamic Mission (UKIM) held its annual conference in Bradford with a morning session devoted to 'Muslim Rights in Britain'. The session was notable for one angry voice dissenting from its general plea for a patient engagement with British institutions, locally and nationally. The Bradford President of Young Muslims UK – then the youth wing of UKIM – fulminated against the preoccupation with 'little rights as a minority'; he poured scorn on the panacea proposed of 'a few Muslims by name in Parliament'. He pointedly reminded the seminar that the Prophet did not labour in Mecca for thirteen years for minority rights but rather to rid society of idolatry and to achieve success in this world and the hereafter. Muslims were in Britain, the land of *kufr*, not to ask for 'petty little things' but to offer the greatest gift, Islam and the Qur'an, a light for all to 'save ourselves and the whole of humanity from the fire'. He bewailed the lack of unity in the community, seduced into competition for state grants, and insisted that God would look after the rights of the community once they behaved like real Muslims. He sought to recall the seminar to the challenge implicit in Islam: guidance for all, a religion of the Book intended 'to prevail over all other ways of life'.[16]

This passionate desire for *da'wa* – to invite others to Islam – and an impatience with the compromises inevitable in any shared life in a democracy point to an abiding dilemma faced by Muslims, especially in a minority situation – a dilemma noted fifty years ago in a seminal work, *Islam in Modern History,* where its author observed that

> *The fundamental malaise of modern Islam is a sense that something has gone wrong with Islamic history. The fundamental problem of modern Muslims is how to rehabilitate that history, to get it going again in full vigour, so that Islamic society may once again flourish as a divinely guided society should and must. The fundamental spiritual crisis in Islam . . . stems from an awareness that something is awry between the religion which God has appointed and the historical development of the world which He controls.*[17]

Writing about Muslims in the secular Republic of India he noted that 'the question of political power and social organization, so central to Islam, has in the past always been considered in yes-or-no terms. Muslims have either had political power or they have not. Never before have they shared it with others.'[18]

While Islamist movements such as the Islamic Society of Britain and UKIM – as well as student groups such as FOSIS – more and more opted for principled engagement throughout the 1990s, groups such as HT continued to resist such compromises and continued to argue for the sort of social, institutional and ideological separatism presupposed by the Muslim Parliament. The leadership, dynamics and style of such groups has been vividly and sympathetically drawn in Hanif Kureishi's novel, *The Black Album* (1995). The central character, a British Pakistani student, Shahid, comes to London where his own identity crisis is played out, torn between twin seductions: post-modernism as represented by his English teacher, Deedee Osgood, and Riaz, the leader of a radical Muslim group.

In the figure of the student leader Riaz, Kureishi communicates and captures the appeal of radical Islam. Riaz's Sunday talks in the mosque

> *were well attended by a growing audience of young people, mostly local . . . Asians. Not being an aged obscurantist, Riaz was becoming the most popular speaker . . . he entitled his talks, 'Rave from the Grave?', 'Adam and Eve not Adam and Steve', 'Islam: A Blast from the Past or a Force for the Future?' and 'Democracy is a Hypocrisy'.*[19]

In an interview with *Newsweek* – subtitled 'Talking to the Next Generation' – Kureishi remarks that he did most of his research 'around colleges of further education' in London. 'I noticed a big change since when I was a student 20 years ago. In my day we were mostly leftists of some variety, but the collapse of Eastern European communism has made that very difficult. Now they are turning to religion.'

As to what drives this return to religion,

> *racism is obviously part of the answer. The point about Islam is that it's not white; it belongs entirely to them. But it's also a way for the kids to save themselves ... against the problems that afflict others. You belong to a rather severe group, you don't take drugs, run around with guns or hang around on the street. Religion gives them a sense of solidarity, of meaning, of hope ... They do feel antagonism to [the white community] after what has been done to them through colonialism and [the imposition of] a kind of materialism that they feel fits them uneasily. Some of them do say that the basic liberalism we take for granted, free speech and democracy are just hypocrisy as far as they are concerned. But the rage against the West often seems to be completely undifferentiated, slapdash and unsophisticated. In fact, there's a mutual construction of an antagonism with Muslims [portrayed] as fanatics and whites as corrupt.*

Such radicalism is not a cohesive movement:

> *A lot of kids hate the mosques, for instance. They hate the mullahs, who they think are corrupt and have the wrong ideas. It certainly isn't as if they were flocking to the mosque to listen to the men of authority. In fact, there are enormous schisms within the community. It reminds me of the Trotskyites in my 20s: there were huge rifts among all the groups, but no one could tell the difference. The tensions are mind-boggling ... Many of the kids I met were kind, sweet and good. At the same time, they [expressed] ideas that made you blanch: homophobia, casual anti-Semitism and so on ... What was so disturbing about the Muslim kids I met was their refusal to think for themselves, their blanket dismissal of the West.*[20]

Until the mid-1990s, much of what passed for radical politics was non-violent, often little more than rhetorical posturing, however uncongenial the ideas expressed. This began to change with the impact of Bosnia and with Britain becoming a haven for 'Arab Afghans' and part of the emerging transnational network of violent jihadis or their spokesmen. The role of Bosnia in giving focus and specificity to what Kureishi calls 'a mutual construction of an antagonism' between Muslims and the West has only recently been recognized.

Bosnia was a shock to British Muslims. Evan Kohlmann, a specialist in this area, points out that 'Bosnia Herzogovina was in Europe and the effect that that had in terms of galvanizing political Islam, of bringing political Islam to the dinner table for British Muslims ... cannot be calculated.'[21] The conflict was inevitably a politicizing event for many young British Muslims, who were appalled that the British government was apparently unwilling either to protect Bosnians or allow them to arm to protect themselves. The suspicions of the UN were reinforced by its failure, brutally exposed with the Srebrenica massacres. Well-integrated European Muslims, blond and blue-eyed, were being ethnically cleansed.

Just at a time when the Afghanistan triumph was being tarnished by intra-ethnic conflict, with Muslim killing Muslim, Bosnia came along, enabling militant Islamists 'to sell the Serb military as the equivalent of the Soviets in Europe – a Christian militia intent on wiping out Muslims'.[22] Such events gave a new lease of life to the rhetoric of such groups as HT, committed in Britain to using such a tragedy to further delegitimize Western democracy and the UN. The conflicts of the mid-1990s in Bosnia, Chechnya and Algeria were all becoming jihadi battlegrounds 'complete with the small backstreet industry of gruesome videos used for recruiting new fighters' or members of radical groups.[23]

London was certainly a magnet for violent jihadis in the late 1990s. In an earlier chapter, the activities of Abu Hamza al-Misri were profiled. He was but one of a small number of Afghan Arabs and apologists for violent jihad who were propagating such ideas and recruiting with relative impunity until 9/11. Two other Wahhabi/Salafi individuals are worth mentioning. The first is Sheikh Abdullah el-Faisal, who merited a full front-page article in *The Times* in February 2002 exposing his energetic promotion of his incendiary videos across the country to Muslim groups, inciting them to kill Jews, Hindus and other 'infidels' and urging the merits of learning to shoot a Kalashnikov as part of compulsory jihad training.[24]

His arrest in February 2002 turned on the fortuitous find of two of his inflammatory tapes – *Jihad* and *The Rules of Jihad* – in the car boot of a motorist arrested in rural Dorset for other offences in December 2001. Investigations found that el-Faisal had been travelling across the country for the previous four years, giving 90-minute addresses to audiences attended by up to 500 people at a time in venues as diverse as Manchester, Birmingham, Coventry, Maidenhead, Bournemouth, Tipton and London.

A convert to Islam in Jamaica, he learned Arabic and earned a degree in Islamic Studies at the Imam Mohammed Ibn Saud Islamic University in the Saudi capital, Riyadh. On instructions from sponsors in Riyadh, el-Faisal came to Britain in 1992, initially worshipping at the Salafi mosque in Brixton, also frequented by the shoe-bomber Richard Reid. Then he moved to Tower Hamlets in East London, where he set up regular study groups. During his four-week trial jurors sat through more than twelve hours of audio and video cassette footage found in specialist Islamic bookshops and at his home.

Although he admitted to translating for Abu Qatada – allegedly a recruiter for Al Qaeda in London – and translating material produced by Usama bin Laden, no direct links with Al Qaeda were discovered. However, he was accused of encouraging Britons to go to terrorist training camps in Afghanistan before and after 9/11. The following brief excerpts from these tapes provide a shocking window into his mind-set:

> *People with British passports, if you fly into Israel it is very easy – no rules. Go and do whatever you can and if you die you will go to paradise.*
>
> *So you can go to India and if you see a Hindu walking down the road you are allowed to kill him and take his money . . . His wealth isn't sacred and nor is his life.*
>
> *Jews are rotten to the core and sexually perverted, creating intrigue and confusion to keep their enemies weak. They should be killed very soon, as by Hitler.*
>
> *You can use chemical weapons to exterminate the unbelievers. Is that clear? If you have cockroaches in your house, you spray them with chemicals.*

In 2003, the 39-year-old was found guilty of soliciting murder and inciting racial hatred and sentenced to eight years' imprisonment. At his trial he defiantly declared that

> *I see it as my duty as a scholar to vigorously defend the Koran and the teachings given to me in accordance with the same at Imam Muhammad Ibn Saud Islamic University in Saudi Arabia. I can only*

> *conclude that the Koran and the Saudi Arabian regime are on trial, since all my teachings are from the Koran and Saudi Arabia.*[25]

The jury were not impressed by such an argument. What is disturbing is that in propagating such hatred, he was able to appeal to his religious credentials as a graduate of a well-known Saudi university. As Deputy Assistant Commissioner Peter Clarke, head of Scotland Yard's Anti-Terrorist Squad, said: 'We simply do not know how many young, impressionable people may have gone abroad and never returned. This case was nothing to do with freedom of speech but everything to do with racial hatred and religious bigotry – and encouraging people to commit acts of terrorism.'[26] His tapes are thought to have influenced the 7/7 bomber Jermaine Lindsay, and were circulating within the Muslim community in High Wycombe, of whom twelve were charged in August 2006 over an alleged plot to blow up airliners over the Atlantic.[27]

What is clear is the damage a small group of activists can wreak. At el-Faisal's trial it became clear that he had links with Abu Hamza al-Misri and Omar Bakri Mohammad, leader of HT in Britain until his break with the movement in 1996, when he created al Muhajirun, which embodied an almost identical ideology.[28] Unsurprisingly, 'several dozen members of *al-Muhajirun* staged protests outside the Old Bailey during the trial, while Abu Hamza also made a supportive appearance'.[29]

A second Wahhabi/Salafi activist has quite a different profile. Dr Muhammad al-Mas'ari is part of a dissenting Saudi Wahhabi movement, critical of their country's invitation to the United States to remove Saddam Hussein from Kuwait during the first Iraq war. In 1994 al-Mas'ari and another Saudi dissident, Saad al-Faqih, established the Committee for Defence of Legitimate Rights [in Saudi Arabia] (CDLR) in London. However, CDLR is no liberal human rights group. The Arabic adjective translated 'legitimate' refers to *sharia* and al-Mas'ari's rendering of it in the Arabic material on their website – unlike the English material – is both anti-Western and rabidly anti-UN for endorsing 'a system of state-based sovereignty that contradicts the universal vision of Islam ... [and] violate[s] Islam by granting equal rights to men and women'. Nor does he endorse 'freedom of belief and freedom of expression outside Islam ... central pillars in the international human rights platform'.[30]

In a 'Five Live Report' broadcast on BBC Radio Five Live in 2004 – 'Islam's Militant Tendency' – Navid Akhtar, with the help of a Saudi exile and human rights activist, Abdul Aziz al-Hamith, discovered that al-Mas'ari's website could best be described as 'a university of terror. An open university for everyone who wants to learn about jihad and be a good jihadi'. It pushed unapologetically an extremist Wahhabi message of 'violent jihad against the enemies of Islam; the belief that Muslims should engage in Holy War'.[31] The Arabic site was once again more extreme than the English one. Al-Mas'ari, now a supporter of the maverick Omar Bakri, voiced his continuing support after 9/11 for Usama bin Laden, whom he had helped set up a London office in the mid-1990s. On the day Akhtar accessed the al-Mas'ari site it had registered almost 10,000 hits. He wondered how many had read the Arabic section that calls for the assassination of Tony Blair!

In the same programme, Akhtar worries about the dozens of bookshops which have sprung up across Britain selling Wahhabi books and DVDs glamorizing jihad and 'espousing an extreme and separatist version of Islam'. Such books feed into a proliferating network of study circles which meet outside the mosques. Akhtar visited such a bookshop – the Maktabah – in Sparkhill, Birmingham, a predominantly Pakistani and Kashmiri area. The store manager showed Akhtar a seven-foot-high set of bookshelves full of different types of books all concerning jihad, including one written by Dhiren Barot, *The Army of Madinah in Kashmir*.

Barot, alias Esa al-Hindi, a Hindu convert, is now serving a life sentence after pleading guilty at the Old Bailey in November 2006 to planning a 'dirty bomb' attack on London. His book accuses Western troops of invading Muslim countries and urges followers to strike back. Three years after the Five Live broadcast, the Maktabah bookshop still stocks Barot's work, along with works 'promoting terrorism, glorifying terrorism and advocating the killing of homosexuals'.[32]

In the light of such an array of incendiary and seditious commentary, the contents of sermons and DVDs in the Wahhabi/Salafi-influenced mosques, especially in Birmingham, that were revealed in the *Dispatches* programme 'Undercover Mosque', first broadcast January 2007, came as little surprise. The programme simply indicated that there were plenty of replacements for the now-imprisoned Abu Hamza al-Misri and Abdullah el-Faisal. They too were preaching virulent anti-Western and anti-democratic sentiments, along with hate-laced invective against Jews and Christians, to the young and not-so-young. The programme profiled preachers peddling an ideology of bigotry and intolerance with roots in Saudi Arabia, illustrated with quotations from the speakers:

1. Allah has created the woman deficient. If she doesn't wear hijab we hit her.
2. Take the homosexual man and throw him from the mountain.
3. You have to live like a state within a state until you take over.
4. The peak, pinnacle, the crest, the summit of Islam is jihad.

There were, however, a few surprises. A Birmingham mosque maintained a two-way video link with scholars in Saudi Arabia whose comments were kept on DVDs. Legal opinions – *fatwa*s – were sought from the Grand Mufti of Saudi Arabia. A Birmingham worshipper puts the following question to him via the video link in 2006:

> *Some people say we shouldn't call Christians and Jews* kuffar *[infidels] and we should establish dialogue and good relations with them. What's your answer to this?*

His answer is uncompromising: 'This is not true, Jews and Christians who do not follow the Prophet Mohammed are *kuffar*. They will go to hell.' He says that Muslims must not help non-believers: 'Anyone who helps or defends an apostate, or a pagan, or an atheist, or anyone who attacks Islam, will be cursed.' The Grand Mufti is later heard saying that children should be hit if they do not pray: 'Tell your children to pray when they are seven, and hit them when they are ten [if they do not].'

Preachers also voice the millenarian fantasy. Abu Usamah, a fiery young American convert, who had already delivered himself of a number of peremptory judgements ranging from the view that the *kuffar* are 'pathological liars' to the notion that apostates from Islam should face exemplary capital punishments of the cruellest sort, finally turns to the coming jihad against the unbelievers:

> *Verily Allah [is] going to bring a group of people that he loves and they love him, these people ... will be soft and kind to the believers and ... rough and tough against the* kuffar, *they will fight the cause of Allah. I encourage all of you to be from amongst them, to begin to cultivate ourselves for the time that is fast approaching when the tables are going to be turned and the Muslims are going to be in a position of being uppermost in strength[.]*[33]

Now, of course, such preachers are careful not to justify 7/7 but they operate from within the same Manichaean world-view. Their selective retrieval of Islamic texts which terrorize the imagination serves to create an atmosphere of expectation and uncertainty. Once again, the preachers can appeal to their Arabic and scholarly credentials gained at Saudi universities. All in all, the sermons and groups reviewed, although often on the wilder shores of Islamic expression, create an environment where young people exposed to such rhetoric can be drawn within the orbit of violent *takfiri* jihadi groups. *Takfiri* means a willingness to label this or that group or Muslim or non-Muslim as a *kafir*, an infidel. Such labelling begins a process of dehumanizing a perceived enemy.

The young men who perpetrated 7/7 or those arrested after 21/7 present themselves as avenging oppressed Muslims across the world on behalf of a universal Muslim community engaged in a transnational battle against the infidels. While only a small minority of Muslims are involved, there are 'indications that many passive or moderate Muslims, some not even religious, do participate in this [ideological] "imaginary": in sentiment, and maybe in token action such as money collections in mosques'.[34]

The mainstream finds its voice: criticizing extremism and 'identity politics'

Paradoxically, 'Undercover Mosque' is a sign of the growing confidence of the Muslim mainstream to face up to and confront a dark side in contemporary expressions of Islam. The programme, after all, included a number of Muslims ready to expose an integral component of the hardline ideology at the core of current terrorism: Saudi-sponsored Wahhabism.

Thus Abdal Hakim Murad, a lecturer in Islamic Studies at Cambridge University and former student chaplain, drew attention to the gravity of the situation: 'I regard what the Saudis are doing in the ghettoes of British Islam as potentially lethal for the future of the community'.

Yahya Birt, on his blog, noted quite properly that the Wahhabi tradition profiled was 'decidedly a minority trend within British Islam', consisting of only some forty-odd mosques. However, he did not sidestep the hard issues raised when he commented that 'it does them no good to persist with a safe public language for non-Muslims and a private hate-filled language for Muslims. One cannot thunder about hating the unbeliever (*kafir*) one moment, and then talk the language of interfaith and multiculturalism the next. If the programme was a set up, it nonetheless revealed a none-too-subtle double-talk at play'.

He rightly pointed out that 'many Salafis, not featured in the programme, have taken a radically different approach since 9/11 and they deserve to be recognised'. But he also argued for the need to be more self-critical about what imams and visiting preachers/lecturers are saying and asked rhetorically: 'How can we expect a balanced form of Islam to emerge from such a hate-filled discourse?'

The core of his complaint was to ask:

> *Why should we put up with the peddling of false dreams of future domination and merely waiting to fight some grand global jihad later on (when the reality is that Muslim countries cannot even secure their own basic sovereignty), of the insecure proclamation of our inherent superiority (surely conditional on our actual conduct), the need to continually demean the* 'kuffar' *(... [such] obsessive hatred reveals something of a fixation akin to attraction), the nasty denigration of women and speaking as if they were in a position to enforce, with relish, the fixed penalties (*hudud*) of Islamic sacred law (rather than as being, as in fact their congregation is, subject to English common law).*[35]

This readiness to face down unacceptable aspects of contemporary Islam is increasingly evident. The website of the Muslim Youth Helpline included an article after 7/7 entitled 'The Terror Within', whose first paragraph read: 'In the wake of the terrorist attacks on London, on Sharm Al Sheikh [the Egyptian holiday resort where three bombs killed 24 holiday-makers in April 2006] and in the light of the daily attacks targeting ordinary Iraqis, many of whom are children, women and elderly people, I found myself asking: is it time to reflect on the beliefs that we hold?'

The article continues in the same candid vein:

> *For decades, the message of hatred has been preached by many imams: hatred to Israel, hatred to America and the West, hatred to the 'infidels' who seek to distort Islam and undermine its message. But in the course of expressing a loathing for Islam's 'enemy', have we lost sight of who the enemy really is, such that it is we who now distort the divine message? I wonder, would the Prophet ... have preached Jihad against people trying to get to work, as in the case*

> *of Londoners last month, or against Iraqi children killed two weeks ago whose only crime was to accept sweets offered by an American soldier?*

The author concludes:

> *The time has come to reflect on the roots of the extremist sects which form the ideological basis for these criminals ... the greatest terror does not come from the Zionist conspiracy, nor from Western infidels, but from within our very communities, in some of the imams that we proclaim as leaders of the ummah, in some of the books that we hold second only to the Holy Qur'an and in some distorted beliefs that we herald as being the message of Allah[.]*[36]

Abdal Hakim Murad, in a wide-ranging essay seeking to make sense of radical Islam, noted that Muslims broadly embody one of three expressions of Islam:

> *Firstly, the 'time capsule' option often embedded in local ethnic particularities, which seeks to preserve the lexicon of faith from any redefinition ...[Secondly,] a 'liberal' option ... which remains an elite option, despite the* de facto *popularity of attenuated and sentimental forms of 'Muslimness' ... the third possibility is to redefine the language of religion to allow it to support identity politics. Religion has, of course, always had the marking of collective and individual identity as one of its functions ... [However, this dimension has] been allowed to expand beyond its natural scope and limits ... the result has often been* a magnification of traditional polarities between the self and the other, *enabled by the steady draining-away of religiously inspired assumptions concerning the universality of notions of honour and decency.*[37]

The roots of contemporary identity politics are complex. Modern society has eroded social hierarchies, where status and 'honour' were relatively fixed, in favour of the rhetoric of equality and human 'dignity'. In a post-Cold War world conflicts of class, ideology and political systems have gradually receded. In their place divisions based on group identities – cultural, ethnic and religious – have assumed a new significance. Democracies have ushered in what has usefully been dubbed 'the politics of recognition', whereby a diversity of groups, cultures and special interests now clamour for equal status and recognition of their identity. With this plea for public recognition goes a demand for resources and representation in policy-making. Muslim identity politics follows in the wake of civil rights in the USA, and gender and sexuality politics.[38]

Many young British Muslims are reacting to what Murad calls the 'time capsule' option of Islam embedded in the imported ethnic specificities of their parents. This was clear in the radio programme already referred to, 'Islam's Militant Tendency'. In seeking to understand why some young Muslim professionals are attracted to an isolationist Wahhabi/Salafi message, Navid Akhtar concluded that they were 'at odds with their parents' insular Asian culture and the mainstream British way of life. They find themselves in a vacuum with no direction, no roots and a lot of questions. "Pure" [Salafi] Islam [presented as the answer] claims to be authentic Islam as practised at the time of the Prophet Muhammad.'[39]

The spread of Wahhabi/Salafi Islam – including radical Islamist versions, and especially on college and university campuses – is partly a result of the failure of mainstream Sunni traditions to connect with young Muslims educated and socialized in Britain. This is clear from the comments of an ex-HT member:

> *HT filled a void for the young intellectually frustrated youth who had been told that Islam is the truth and they must pray and fast by people who couldn't explain why. [With] HT 'proving' that Freedom, Democracy and Capitalism are defective, and that we Muslims are better than those kaffirs, it restored some of the loss of faith in the relevance of religion. Muslims believe in Islam but needed to know that their belief was the superior belief, which made them feel superior again. Constant harping back to the glory days of the Caliphate and emphasising its restoration as the solution to all things seemed alluring.*[40]

Membership of such groups can meet any number of functions: with regard to external, non-Muslim society it can act as a shield against prejudice and Islamophobia, an act of defiance against an imagined Western monolith intent on subverting Islam, a home for wannabe utopian radicals orphaned by the collapse of far left politics; internally, it can be a protest against a traditionalist, patriarchal community and a religious leadership considered irrelevant. However, in the long term, whenever religion becomes ideology it ceases to satisfy. For many the gap between party rhetoric and actual practice can become insupportable. As an ex-member commented:

> *I could not reconcile our anti-kufr stance with most of my HT friends and their love of their designer labels and their materialistic outlook on life. I could not reconcile the fact that one of my acquaintances worked for a large bank in the city; the very* ribawi *[usurious] institution that HT purportedly stood against.*[41]

As another commentator wryly remarks, 'much like invocations of Marxist utopias advanced by the radical left in Europe, the articulation of utopian Islamic visions is a badge of moral virtue which does not necessarily imply a serious willingness to give up the material comforts of bourgeois society'.[42]

An Arab scholar of Islamic law now working in the USA, Professor Khaled Abou El Fadl, has penned a damaging critique of Wahhabi/Salafi Islam and its negative impact on the West, in a widely reproduced article entitled 'The Theology of Power'. In it he claims that movements such as HT, while influenced by national liberation and anti-colonial struggles, also draw on a Wahhabi/Salafi perspective at once 'puritan, supremacist and thoroughly opportunistic'.[43] Such a movement seeks to resist 'the indeterminacy of the modern age by escaping to a strict literalism in which the text became the sole source of legitimacy.' The majority of Islamic history is dismissed as a corruption of true and authentic Islam. With this dismissal goes a rejection of Sufism and the intellectual monuments of Islamic civilization. In its place, Salafism posits a golden age in the past, 'an historical utopia that can be reproduced in contemporary Islam'. Unsurprisingly, it remains uninterested in critical historical enquiry or the need to interpret divine law contextually.

Instead of scholarship, Salafism responds to the challenges of modernity with 'pious fictions'. The apologetic imagination goes into overdrive, claiming that any worthwhile modern institution was first invented by Muslims, that 'Islam liberated women, created democracy, endorsed pluralism, protected human rights ... before these institutions ever existed in the West'. Such apologetics contributes to 'a sense of intellectual self-sufficiency that often descended into moral arrogance. To the extent that apologetics were habit-forming, it produced a culture that eschewed self-critical and introspective insight, and embraced the projection of blame and [a] fantasy-like level of confidence'.[44]

The problem is that these pious fictions have been projected world-wide through massive Saudi funding. A recent study estimated

'Saudi spending on religious causes abroad as between $2 billion and $3 billion per year since 1975 (comparing favourably with what was the annual Soviet propaganda budget of $1 billion), which has been spent on 1,500 mosques, 210 Islamic centres and dozens of Muslim academies and schools'.

In Britain this entails the flooding of the Islamic book market with cheap, well-produced Salafi literature 'whose print runs can be five to ten times that of any other British-based sectarian publication, aggressively targeted for a global English-speaking audience'. This can have the effect of putting out of business smaller bookshops catering for a more mainstream Muslim market. At the centre of this global movement is the Islamic University of Medina, which 'boasts of having over 5,000 students from 139 countries ... 85 per cent of its places [allocated] to non-Saudis ... The first British-born graduates ... began to return home during the 1980s. In total, British graduates from Medina number in the hundreds'.[45]

This expression of Muslim identity politics increasingly 'thrives through romantic, global solidarities as wars and massacres in Palestine, Bosnia, Kosovo, the Gulf, Chechnya, Kashmir, India, and so on fill our newspapers and television screens and lead some young British-born Muslims to reinvent the concept of the *umma*, the global community of Muslims, as global victims'. [46] This can translate into either isolating Muslim communities from wider society or defining Muslim communities in terms oppositional to Western society, with democracy dismissed as part of *kufr* society, the route taken by HT.

The numbers involved in both HT and its breakaway body – al Muhajirun – are relatively modest. The larger group is HT, with estimates for active membership of between five and eight thousand. In 2003 it could attract between six and seven thousand to a major gathering in London.[47] Al Muhajirun is much smaller. In its heyday, it had 'branches in thirty cities ... 160 "formal members", 700 followers [who] take weekly religious lessons ... [and] an estimated 7,000 "contacts" ... potential participants in their events'.[48]

Whatever the complex reasons advanced for the popularity of such movements, ex-members as well as critics realize that their popularity will only be eroded if practical alternatives exist for constructively channelling often legitimate disquiet within the Muslim communities with patterns of social exclusion, Islamophobia in Britain, or the negative impact of Western foreign policy.

Beyond victimhood

There are many examples of how British Muslims are resisting the seductive allure of a culture of mere complaint. These have taken many forms. The isolationist option of the Muslim Parliament was resisted by a policy of engagement pursued by the Muslim Council of Britain, whatever its structural weaknesses. Many Muslims joined the Stop the War movement, despite HT strictures about joining the *kuffar*! While some commentators are sceptical about the political movement Respect, which they see as an unstable marriage of the far left and Muslim anti-war groups, nonetheless it operates within a democratic framework, as does the political lobby group, MPACUK (the Muslim Public Affairs Committee UK). Muslim communities have also generated development and aid agencies, such as Islamic Relief, respected among fellow-professionals in the field, with whom they now work collaboratively. These are practical ways of addressing some of the real concerns about poverty across large swathes of the Muslim world.

This book has showcased many positive initiatives by young British Muslim professionals who have a stake in Britain and want to address a range of difficult issues internal to the communities. However, as Abdal Hakim Murad observes, 'the medicine for terrorism [and, we might add, for groups such as HT] must be supplied from within the community, and within the theological resources of Islam. Sociological explanations outline circumstances, but cannot disclose the religious underpinnings of these aberrations, or offer counter-argument.'[49]

Three brief examples will be offered of attempts to undercut the appeal of radicalism, one from within traditional Islam, another from within the Islamist tradition, and the third combining a range of perspectives, whether Sufi, modernist or Islamist.

Sheikh Musa Admani, now in his mid-forties, is an East African Muslim of Indian background who completed his *'alim* education at the celebrated Deoband 'seminary' in India. After a period as an imam in a London mosque in the 1990s, he was appointed Muslim chaplain to a London university a few years ago. From both vantage points, Musa watched with anxiety the radicalization of sections of British Muslims in London and the deepening hostility to the West many British Muslim professionals evinced. As a university chaplain he has sought to address the issue of radicalism head on.

From the start of his appointment there was a concerted attempt by HT to delegitimize him, as well as physically threaten him. In all, he has patiently worked to isolate them on campus, enjoying the full support of the university administration and fellow-chaplains. This he has sought to do by making sure that all Muslim groups on campus are represented on a chaplaincy advisory board – not simply the Islamic Society, which has often been hijacked by one or other radical and sectarian group. Further, he has developed written guidelines both for visiting speakers and for those delivering the *khutba* (sermon) on Friday which could well become models for other Muslim university chaplains.[50]

These guidelines provide an insight into both the feverish ideological and sectarian world of Muslim student politics and how one imam, willing to engage with such a world, can begin to challenge its paranoia, in part by addressing the language in which issues are framed. Any would-be campus mosque speaker has to negotiate various hurdles: first, they have to provide two references which attest to the speaker's standing and experience; they must also adhere to university rules and conform to equal opportunities policy, and enhance 'mutual respect and understanding'.

The guidelines for the Friday *khutba* remind the invitee that students are drawn from many different traditions and so it is important 'to respect other people's *madhabs* [legal schools] and personalities by not … attacking them directly or indirectly'; 'controversial issues must be avoided'; speakers must not 'incite hatred or violence in their talks … If one disagrees with a particular *madhab* or school of thought [this] is not the time to air it'; 'words that have become symbols of hate, such as *kuffar*, *dajjal* [anti-Christ], *taghut* [idols] and pagan systems of rule, should be substituted … with alternatives such as people of other faith, non-Muslims etc. … It is important to avoid denigrating remarks about university education in preference to other ways of learning … Speakers should not [seek] to recruit students to their causes.'

Musa was concerned at hearing Islamic vocabulary, rooted in the Qur'an and Prophetic example, routinely torn out of context and misapplied in such a way as to suggest binary worlds of 'us' and 'them'. Jihad was misunderstood and romanticized to legitimize terror. Christians and Jews were seldom referred to by the correct Qur'anic term, *Ahl al-Kitab*, People of the Book, but demonized through the use of the pejorative *kuffar*. Similarly, the West was essentialized as a pagan system over and against an imagined perfect Islamic system.

To address such issues, he has given serious study of the Qur'an pride of place in the religious teaching he offers students. To this end, he has started an innovative weekly Qur'an study session among his university students on campus, to help them engage with the text directly. Finally, he has used such experience as part of his work with his charity – the Luqman Institute of Education and Development. Its work in tackling the effects of indoctrination by sending volunteers to campuses to challenge such views has been profiled in the national press:

> *Up to 10 students [at a university in London] are being 'deradicalised' by a caseworker from the Institute. Jawad Syed, who nearly succumbed to extremism himself . . . said: 'Some of the students are watching jihadi videos . . . and listening to different sheikhs encouraging jihad'.*[51]

When the government established its seven 'Preventing Extremism Together' (PET) working parties in the aftermath of 7/7, it included Dr Tariq Ramadan, grandson of the founder of the Muslim Brotherhood (MB). There is a certain irony here: his grandfather spent most of his life confronting British colonialism – not least what we might call the 'colonization of the mind' – while his grandson is invited by the British government to help address extremism within the Muslim communities, an extremism frequently blamed on imported ideologies such as the radical end of MB!

Ramadan, who spent 2005/6 as a visiting fellow at St Anthony's College in Oxford University, describes himself as Muslim by religion, Swiss by nationality, European by culture, Egyptian by memory and a Universalist by principle – i.e. he seeks to embody Islamic principles considered universal.[52] His most recent work – *Western Muslims and the Future of Islam* – represents one of the most sustained efforts yet to 'find out how the Islamic universal accepts and respects pluralism and the belief of the Other'.[53] It is an imaginative work and his talks are characterized by the same boldness.

In an address he gave at Bradford University he was critical of the 'obsession with a Muslim identity'. This was understandable twenty years ago, he averred, but now that we are 'at home' here, we need to develop the 'values and principles' to discern the good from the bad both in British culture and in the inherited culture of parents. He urged a 'committed and critical citizenship' and was impatient with the naivety of literalist Salafis who told British Muslims not to engage in democratic politics since they cannot discern it in the Prophetic practice (*Sunna*) – not realizing this is already a form of politics, namely silent support for the status quo. He chided Muslims for sending their *zakat* (alms tax) to the needy overseas while forgetting 'the poor around you'. In the question-and-answer session he sought to clarify the relationship of ethics to Islamic law.

He mentioned that he was working on a new book about the principles of Islamic jurisprudence. Such a world was not a closed landscape. However, classical scholars, he maintained, had been 'concerned with the imposition of law not with values and context'. Therefore, 'we need to recover values and be alert to context. This presupposed a role for non-textual scholars to be part of a joint *ijtihad*, scholarly effort, to apply texts to new situations.' He criticized Muslims for their laziness: many Muslim scholars speak about the West without knowledge of its history, culture and context. His talk exuded the same bracing air as his book, where he warned Muslims in the West to avoid 'self-ghettoization', becoming 'spectators in a society where they were once marginalized'. They also had to let go of 'an idealized history of Islamic civilization' and its corollary, 'a patent lack of self-criticism'.[54]

Here is an influential voice, in some respects post-Islamist, acceptable in moderate Islamist circles. He indicates how the tradition is developing in the West. Where once Islamists aimed to create a new world, rather than improve the one people actually lived in, they have begun to shift from a transformative rhetoric – what I have dubbed a utopian politics – to an ameliorative politics.

This is clear in his remarks to an annual forum the *Guardian* newspaper organizes for some sixty young Muslims from across the country. Madeleine Bunting, who covered the event, drew attention to the fact that,

> *Steeped in a French republican tradition of strong citizenship, he is remarkably challenging of his Muslim audiences. Who else can talk about the passivity and victim mentality of the Muslim community . . . and still get spontaneous applause? Who else challenges the community to stop complaining about not being consulted by the government, but organise themselves so effectively that the government has no choice but to listen? Who else argues that if Muslims want British-trained imams, they'll have to pay for them instead of donating to international solidarity campaigns? You can best help the oppressed around the world by being a good citizen here, he stoutly commented. This is tough love, and it is to the considerable credit of his audience that they want it.*[55]

The final example of a considered attempt to undercut the appeal of violent extremism is a project which emerged from PET, the Radical Middle Way (RMW). The aim of RMW is to draw on the best of contemporary scholarship from across the Muslim world to present a robust and relevant vision for young British Muslims. It is a partnership of government and groups with roots in the student and young adult community. Wherever the roadshow has toured, it has played to packed groups. At a recent meeting in Bradford – on the theme 'From Protest to Engagement' – it attracted some 1,200 young people.

It is a rewarding experience to access their website and to download a wealth of insightful talks.[56] There is a particularly moving question-and-answer session around the theme 'After Genocide – Islam, Social Justice and the Power of Reconciliation'. This involved three scholars – Mufti Mustafa Ceric (Bosnia and Herzegovina), Mufti Saleh Habiman (Rwanda) and Naeem Jinnah (South Africa). Young people listened with rapt attention to the two muftis from Bosnia and Rwanda explain how Islam gave them the capacity to build a new society after the trauma of ethnic cleansing and systemic genocide.

The website also includes an article by Fareena Alam, the editor of *Q-News* – 'Why I Reject the Anarchists Who Claim to Speak for Islam', reproduced from the *Observer* newspaper. In it, she introduces some of the other RMW speakers: Abdullah bin Bayyah, one of Sunni Islam's greatest living jurists, from the West African nation of Mauritania; Hamza Yusuf, to whom frequent reference has already been made; and Zaid Shakir. Alam cites some remarks by Shakir which were well received:

> *'We must stop thinking of ourselves as "the tribe of Islam", declared Imam Zaid Shakir, an African-American scholar and civil rights activist. 'Until we start to think of ourselves as the children of Adam, concerned about the welfare of all our fellow human beings, we are missing the point of being faithful. These are days [in the wake of the Danish cartoons controversy] when there is a lot of talk about defending the honour of the Prophet. What would it do for the honour of the Prophet if Muslims mobilised their tremendous resources to eradicate hunger from this planet? What would it say to the world if Muslims mobilised to end the conflict in the Congo or to make generic Aids drugs available where they are not?' The crowd burst into enthusiastic applause.*[57]

What was impressive about the meeting I attended was the variety of speakers from a range of ethnic groups. Also, interwoven with addresses of varying length, there was plenty of music, similarly international, which included a local Yorkshire Islamic rapper, beautiful traditional devotional songs from North Africa and a guest appearance from Sami Yusuf. It embodied an appeal to conscience, creativity and compassion – the three themes increasingly important to the young journalists of *Q-News* mentioned in an earlier chapter. Unsurprisingly, *Q-News* is one of the main organizers, along with two organizations which have roots in the student communities, FOSIS and YMOUK (Young Muslim Organisation United Kingdom). This partnership is also significant because it encompasses Sufi and moderate Islamist groups, which suggests a cure for imported antagonisms.

Notes

1. Quotations and paraphrases of Shiraz Maher are based on two of his articles: 'I was a Student on the Frontline', the *Times Higher Educational Supplement*, 27 October 2006, p. 19, and an overlapping account, 'Modes and Methods: How Extremists Recruit in Modern Britain', taken from the published report of a conference organized by an NGO, Policy Spotlight Ltd, on 5 December 2006, 'Engaging with Young Muslim Men at Risk of Exclusion', pp. 11–17 (report privately circulated, n.d.).

2. My account of Fatima Khan's story is taken from Navid Akhtar's Channel 4 film, *Young, Angry and Muslim*, first broadcast 24 October 2005.

3. Spoken on a BBC Radio 4 *Analysis* programme devoted to 'Koran and Country: How Islam Got Political', first broadcast 10 November 2005.

4. P. Werbner, 'The Predicament of Diaspora and Millennial Islam: Reflections on September 11, 2001', *Ethnicities*, 4 (2004), p. 468. I am indebted to this seminal article for its suggestive remarks about utopianism/millenarianism in contemporary Islam.

5. R. Hassan, *Faithlines: Muslim Conceptions of Islam and Society* (Oxford: Oxford University Press, 2002), p. 222. The other countries in the survey were Egypt, Indonesia and Kazakhstan.

6. Ibid., p. 217.

7. Werbner, 'The Predicament of Diaspora and Millennial Islam', p. 468.

8. P. Werbner, *Imagined Diasporas among Manchester Muslims* (Oxford: James Curry, 2002), p. 157.

9. Ibid., pp. 162–3.

10. Ibid., p. 183. For more examples see Werbner, *Imagined Diasporas*, pp. 457–8.

11. See Z. Sardar, *Desperately Seeking Paradise: Journeys of a Sceptical Muslim* (London: Granta, 2004), esp. ch. 9, 'The Heavenly Revolution'.

12. See ibid., ch. 2, 'The Brotherhood of Salvation'.

13. Remarks from the Radio 4 programme, 'Koran and Country'.

14. P. Lewis, *Islamic Britain: Religion, Politics and British Muslims*, 2nd edn (London: I. B. Tauris, 2002), pp. 52–3.

15. 'I think political Islam – the road it

has put us on is a road of destruction. I think today, as a result of this approach, we are against everybody. We simply cannot afford to have the whole world against us ... Every ... idea we have is based on some kind of a confrontation and I think the time has come that Muslims wake up and challenge these dangerous ideas', 'Koran and Country'.

16. Lewis, *Islamic Britain*, p. 175.

17. W. C. Smith, *Islam in Modern History* (New York: New American Library, 1957), pp. 47–8.

18. Ibid., p. 286.

19. H. Kureishi, *The Black Album* (London: Faber and Faber, 1995), p. 80.

20. H. Kureishi, 'Sweet Kids with Shocking Ideas', *Newsweek*, 29 May 1995, p. 17.

21. 'Koran and Country'. See E. Kohlmann, *Al-Qaida's Jihad in Europe: The Afghan Bosnian Network* (Oxford: Berg, 2004).

22. Evan Kohlmann, on 'Koran and Country'.

23. Frank Gardner, ibid.

24. 'Britain's sheikh of race hatred', *The Times*, 4 February 2002.

25. 'Koran is on trial, sheikh says as he is denied bail', *The Times*, 22 February 2002.

26. 'Muslim Cleric is Convicted of Soliciting Murder', *The Times*, 25 February 2003. I have drawn on this and an earlier *Times* article on 23 January 2003, entitled 'Imam "Instructed British Muslims to Kill Infidels"', for further background.

27. See 'Half of Terror Plot Suspects to be Charged', *The Sunday Times*, 20 August 2006.

28. See the outstanding study by Q. Wiktorowicz, *Radical Islam Rising: Muslim Extremism in the West* (Lanham, Md: Rowman and Littlefield, 2005).

29. 'Profile: El-Faisal, the Sheikh of Race Hate', *The Times*, 24 February 2003.

30. See M. Fandy, *Saudi Arabia and the Politics of Dissent* (New York: St Martin's Press, 1999), pp. 138, 140.

31. 'Islam's Militant Tendency', first broadcast on Radio Five Live, 14 March 2004.

32. 'Bookshop's Message of Racist Hate', *The Observer*, 4 February 2007.

33. Quotations and paraphrases of the 'Undercover Mosque' programme are based on a transcript made by MPACUK, the Muslim Public Affairs Committee UK.

34. S. Zubaida, 'London Bombs: Iraq or the "Rage of Islam"?', <www.opendemocracy.net>, accessed 3 August 2005.

35. 'Uncovering "Undercover Mosque"', <www.yahyabirt.com>, accessed 25 February 2007.

36. 'The Terror Within', <www.muslimyouth.net>, accessed 23 December 2006.

37. Tim Winter (the English name of Abdal Hakim Murad), 'Muslim Loyalty and Belonging: Some Reflections on the Psychosocial Background', in M. Seddon (ed.), *British Muslims: Loyalty and Belonging* (Leicester: Islamic Foundation, 2003), pp. 5–6, italics mine.

38. See especially the classic text by C. Taylor, *Multiculturalism and the 'Politics of Recognition'* (Princeton: Princeton University Press, 1992), and also T. Modood, *Multicultural Politics: Racism, Ethnicity and Muslims in Britain* (Edinburgh: Edinburgh University Press, 2005).

39. 'Islam's Militant Tendency'.

40. S. Hamid, 'Islamic Political Radicalism in Britain: The Case of Hizb-ut-Tahrir', in T. Abbas (ed.), *Islamic Political Radicalism: A European Perspective* (Edinburgh: Edinburgh University Press, 2007), p. 150.

41. Quoted ibid., p. 154.

42. Werbner, 'The Predicament of Diaspora and Millennial Islam', p. 455.

43. First published in *Middle East Report*, 222 (Winter 2001). The version I am citing appeared as 'Islam and the Theology of Power', in A. A. Malik (ed.), *With God On Our Side: Politics and Theology of the War on Terrorism* (Bristol: Amal Press, 2005), pp. 299–311.

44. Ibid., pp. 304–10.

45. J. Birt, 'Wahhabism in the United Kingdom: Manifestations and Reactions', in M. Al-Rasheed (ed.), *Transnational Connections and the Arab Gulf* (London: Routledge, 2005), pp. 169, 170–1.

46. Modood, *Multicultural Politics*, p. 160.

47. See Hamid, 'Islamic Political Radicalism in Britain', p. 156. I have checked with a number of specialists on HT who proffer these estimates.

48. Wiktorowicz, *Radical Islam Rising*, p. 10.

49. A. H. Murad, 'Islam's "Heart of Darkness"', *The Tablet*, 23 July 2005, p. 4.

50. I am grateful to Sheikh Admani for giving me a copy of these guidelines in 2004 (undated, no pagination).

51. 'Islamists Infiltrate Four Universities', *The Sunday Times*, 12 November 2006.

52. This is how he described himself in a talk he gave at Bradford University to launch the annual Islam Awareness Week organized by the Islamic Society of Britain (ISB), 21 November 2005.

53. T. Ramadan, *Western Muslims and the Future of Islam* (Oxford: Oxford University Press, 2004), pp. 5–6.

54. Ibid., p. 55.

55. M. Bunting, 'Why Muslims Must Guard Against the Satisfactions of Complaint', *Guardian*, 21 November 2005.

56. See <www.radicalmuslimway.co.uk>.

57. F. Alam, 'Why I Reject the Anarchists Who Claim to Speak For Islam', *The Observer*, 12 February 2006.

Conclusion

The phrase 'young British Muslims' clearly encompasses a complex reality. Young Muslims are embedded in a huge diversity of ethnic communities. With regard to young Turks and Kurds in London, it can be Pakistani children in the schoolroom who make fun of their poor English. Unlike those of Pakistani background, whose religiosity is more visible, what with beards and hijabs, Turks and Kurds tend to experience more anti-Turkish hostility than anti-Muslim prejudice. When a couple of English fans were killed after a football match in Istanbul, London's Turkish community was exposed to some abuse.[1]

Within the largest Muslim communities in Britain – those with roots in Pakistan – there are huge differences between rural Kashmiris and urban Punjabis. The gritty reality of inner-city Bradford, the backcloth for M. Y. Alam's novel *Kilo*, is to be found amidst a community largely from rural Kashmir. This is very different from the elegant social world of the successful urban Punjabi restaurant 'tribes', whose cut-throat rivalries in Manchester's Curry Mile are amusingly dissected in Zahid Hussain's recent novel of that name.

Policy-makers worry about the existence of 'parallel worlds', especially in northern cities. Whatever the precise nature, extent, reasons for and significance of such social, cultural and spatial separation, it is clear that young Muslims within those spaces consider themselves British and share many aspects of popular youth culture with their non-Muslim peers.[2] Their problem is with the many traditionally-minded parents who seek, usually unsuccessfully, to limit their access to it.

One of the strengths of Hussain's novel, which traces the fortunes and inter-generational tensions of Ajmal, 'Curry King' and old-time patriarch, and his unruly family, is Ajmal's dawning realization that discrete Pakistani and English social and cultural worlds – 'ours' (*apne*) and 'theirs' (*goray*) – no longer exist for their children. Indeed, at the end of the book, Ajmal and a bitter business rival from a different clan, Jafar Ali, both speak of their 'goray children'.[3] They have come to realize that their children refuse to allow parental rivalries to stand in the way of their personal friendship. Clan honour has lost much of its constraining power with a new generation of educated British Pakistanis.

What is clear, however, is that for many parents, community elders, and religious leaders, disentangling religion from culture is not so easy. In many ways this is where the battle lines are being drawn. Many educated young Muslims, especially women, are increasingly appealing to Islam to criticize aspects of imported parental culture, felt to be oppressive and dysfunctional. No aspect of traditional culture is more contested than transcontinental marriage with rural cousins. Too often this is seen as serving to consolidate clan loyalties rather than serving the interests of the young people themselves.

With regard to Islam and young Muslims, the latter are

> *searching for a form of Islam that makes sense in a multicultural context. They find it hard to get answers, particularly where they rely on imams from overseas who don't speak English. Imams should be giving young people tools to integrate on their own terms. Too often they have tended to say 'Live at peace with your neighbours' and at the same time, 'We don't want to live like them'. So the message has been, 'Be good but be separate'.*[4]

A recent contribution on the radicalization of young Muslims rightly noted that '*there is no natural continuum from radical Muslim to militant violence.* Radical Muslims variously preach their practice, establish independent institutions like schools, rage against oppression, argue about forms of Muslim governance or the correct practice of the religion'.[5] However, these same radicals know that 'they need this open British society to have the freedom to do all these things. Even in their most impassioned moments, they are still doing so inside this society, not outside it ... as outlaws.'[6]

A few fail to make the distinction between 'radical stakeholder and militant nihilist', partly because Muslim elders are unable to offer appropriate guidance:

> *if they respond at all it is to shut the trouble-makers out instead of guiding them in. Usually they are altogether unaware of the dangers because there never has been a channel for communication* – traditional Muslim associations have no concept of rebellious youth.[7]

This void has been filled by a proliferation of initiatives documented in this book, ranging from an informal school for Muslim journalism, to helplines and the creation of a youth foundation for Muslim young people, to a citizenship course for mosque and school. These few examples are indicative rather than exhaustive of the creativity of a new generation of young British Muslim professionals who, weary of the paralysis of many of their elders, have independently sought to plug the gaping holes in provision.

What is also evident is a new self-criticism and humour apparent in Muslim publications – both of which are marks of growing self-confidence. I have in front of me a recent edition of a beautifully produced Muslim lifestyle magazine, *Emel*. It includes a regular column with the catchy title, 'Diary of a Desperate Dad', another concerned with 'Ethics', and a balanced and generous review of the autobiography by the controversial Dutch Somali female MP Ayaan Hirsi Ali, with the provocative title *Infidel: The Story of My Enlightenment*. An article is also devoted to a spate of works urging the need for a reformation in Islam, and includes the following comment:

> *I would like my children to know that debate is healthy; to be exposed to discussion, to see it as normal and enriching. What I do not want is for them to be straight-jacketed into a rigid doctrine where they are forbidden to dissent. Groups like the Progressive Muslims strike a chord in lamenting our lost heritage of questioning; the ethos of searching and reasoning that lies dormant.*[8]

Reading this fine publication, it is clear that as with *Q-News*, the editor, along with many of its contributors, are women. British Muslim women are finding their voice. As with many of their male peers, they are looking for expansive readings of the Islamic tradition which make possible and legitimize a constructive conversation between their multiple identities. This is the challenge for Islamic scholarship in general and the world of the mosque in particular. It is interesting that many Muslims are looking outside South Asia and the Middle East to Europe. They are retrieving moments in European history where Muslim, Christian and Jew co-existed, whether in Spain or the Ottoman Empire. Bosnian Islamic scholars are being sought out, since they represent a sophisticated European expression of Islam.

In general, British Muslims are beginning to press for a principled engagement with all aspects of British society rather than staying within their comfort zones. It is important that wider society respond with equal generosity. Not least, policy-makers should be ready to give space, time and, where necessary, resources to enable this engagement to deepen and bear fruit.

Muslims in Britain at ease Islamically with religious diversity and democracy, making their distinctive contributions to public and civic debate as citizens, could have a huge contribution to the same debates across the Muslim world. After all, in Britain, unlike much of the Muslim world, there is intellectual freedom and space for robust debate. However, as the Muslim scholar Tariq Ramadan reminds us, 'the Road is still long ... one must not be afraid or apologize for needing time.'[9]

Notes

1. P. Enneli, T. Modood and H. Bradley, *Young Turks and Kurds: A Set of 'Invisible' Disadvantaged Groups* (York: Joseph Rowntree Foundation, 2005), pp. 30, 42.

2. An excellent way in to the debates around such issues is an article by Alan Carling, 'The Curious Case of the Mis-claimed Myth Claims: Ethnic Segregation, Polarization and the Future of Bradford', forthcoming in *Urban Studies*.

3. Z. Hussain, *The Curry Mile* (London: Suitcase Books, 2006), p. 275. I am grateful to a Mancunian friend, Sadek Hamid, for drawing my attention to this novel. 'Goray' literally means 'white' but carries the meaning of 'their', rather than 'our', social and cultural world.

4. Y. Birt, 'Do You Want a Muslim Neighbour?', <www.flintoff.org/article/208/do-you-want-a-muslim-neighbour>, accessed 23 December 2006.

5. M. Naqshbandi, *Problems and Practical Solutions to Tackle Extremism Problems; and Muslim Youth and Community Issues*, The Shrivenham Papers, no. 1 (Shrivenham, Oxon.: Defence Academy of the United Kingdom, 2006), p. 8, italics mine.

6. Ibid.

7. Ibid., italics mine.

8. S. Saigol, 'Talking about a Reformation', *Emel*, 31 (April 2007), p. 20.

9. T. Ramadan, *Western Muslims and the Future of Islam* (Oxford: Oxford University Press, 2004), p. 7.

A Brief Annotated Bibliography

This book is not intended as a primer on Islam and I am conscious that some issues have been ignored altogether. The following monographs and websites seek to signpost a few studies and resources which I have found stimulating – studies, in addition to those already mentioned in the notes, which can contribute to a more generous framework in which to locate the British component of a significant new chapter in a long encounter between Muslims and the West.

Abou El Fadl, K., *The Great Theft: Wrestling Islam from the Extremists* (New York: HarperSanFrancisco, 2005). El Fadl is probably the finest Sunni scholar of Islamic law writing in the USA today. He explores contemporary issues as disputed between Wahhabis and the moderates: gender, morality, attitudes to non-Muslims, human rights, democracy and attitudes to history.

Ahmad, I., *Unimagined: A Muslim Boy Meets the West* (London, Aurum Press, 2007). A whimsical memoir of growing up in London and attending university in Scotland. Also an unofficial manifesto for British Muslims for Secular Democracy, of which Ahmad is a trustee.

Aslan, R., *No God But God: The Origins, Evolution and Future of Islam* (London: Arrow Books, 2006). A readable and critical short history of Islam by an Iranian novelist and scholar now resident in the USA, offering a perspective that is alert to Shi'ite Islam. Includes a very useful bibliography.

Bianchi, R., *Guests of God: Pilgrimage and Politics in the Islamic World* (Oxford: Oxford University Press, 2004). A beautifully written and exhaustively researched study of pilgrimage and how politicians and generals across the Muslim world use access to pilgrimage to reward their supporters. A *tour d'horizon* of the contemporary Muslim world. Here one discovers that 'London has become the hajj capital of Europe' (p. 63).

Bulliet, W., *The Case for Islamo-Christian Civilization* (New York: Columbia University Press, 2006). Note the title! A robust critique of the fashionable 'clash of civilizations' argument which postulates inevitable conflict between the West and the world of Islam. This timely work is by one of the USA's finest historians of the Islamic world.

Cesari, J., and McLoughlin, S. (eds), *European Muslims and the Secular State* (Aldershot: Ashgate, 2005). A good comparative study of Muslims in a range of European countries.

Cook, D., *Understanding Jihad* (London: University of California Press, 2005). An accessible study which cuts through myths about jihad and traces how understandings have changed across Muslim history.

Ernst, C., and Lawrence, B., *Sufi Martyrs of Love: The Chishti Order in South Asia and Beyond* (London: PalgraveMacmillan, 2002). A readable study of a major Indo-Pakistan Sufi order which indicates the historical importance of this tradition of Islam and its continuing relevance as a custodian of Islamic humanism.

Goodman, L., *Islamic Humanism* (Oxford: Oxford University Press, 2003). A marvellous antidote to contemporary politicized discourses stressing Muslim victimhood. These essays, the fruit of forty years of engagement with Islam, remind Muslims that they are heirs of an earlier expansive Islamic civilization which produced poetry, ethics and philosophy in dialogue with Jewish, Christian and other civilizations.

Husain, E., *The Islamist: Why I Joined Radical Islam in Britain, What I Saw Inside and Why I Left* (London: Penguin, 2007). A controversial ex-member's perspective on radicalism.

Irwin, R., *The Lust for Knowing: The Orientalists and their Enemies* (London: Penguin, 2006). A *tour de force* of intellectual history charting the origins and heyday of Orientalism – the study of the Middle East and Near East – enlivened by an array of sketches of memorable characters. A rejoinder to dismissive and reductionist accounts of their labours.

Kepel, G., *The War for Muslim Minds: Islam and the West* (Cambridge, Mass.: Belknap Press of Harvard University, 2004). A fine overview of the dynamics and genealogy of global terrorism, with incisive commentary on the USA, Saudi Arabia, Iraq and Muslims in Europe by one of France's leading scholars of violent Islamism.

Peters, F. E., *Muhammad and the Origins of Islam* (Albany, NY: State University of New York Press, 1994). An excellent and accessible biography of the Prophet which is neither pietistic nor polemical, including a helpful appendix, 'The Quest of the Historical Muhammad'.

Solomon, N., Harries, R., and Winter, T. (eds), *Abraham's Children: Jews, Christians and Muslims in Conversation* (London: T. & T. Clark, 2005). The Oxford Abrahamic Group has been meeting for more than ten years. This is the fruit of their scholarly interaction, clarifying similarities and differences and ways forward to develop trust and co-operation.

Werbner, P., *Pilgrims of Love: The Anthropology of a Global Sufi Cult* (London: Hurst and Co., 2004). A landmark study of a transnational Sufi network whose headquarters is in Pakistan, with a major centre in Birmingham.

A good point of entry for understanding the range of expressions of contemporary Islam is to visit a range of websites of particular traditions.

For traditional Islam:

<www.inter-islam.org> is the main Deobandi website produced at the Bury 'seminary'.

<www.FatwaIslam.com> is a Salafi website.

<www.masud.co.uk> is a good Sunni/Sufi website with lots of links.

<www.islam-online.net> is a Islamist website which provides many interesting articles by the influential Egyptian scholar Yusuf al-Qaradawi, now based in Qatar.

<http://godlas.myweb.uga.edu> is an academic website developed by an American Muslim scholar, with many excellent sections having many good link sites on 'Islam in the Modern World' and 'Islamic History', as well as some basic material on Islamic sciences.

Blogs are also a way in to contemporary debate and commentary:

<www.eteraz.org> is one of the best, which includes a list of other blogs.

<www.yahyabirt.com/> provides stimulating and thoughtful commentary on a range of contentious issues.

<www.opendemocracy.net> provides some of the most reflective debate on different aspects of Islam in Britain.

For those interested in interfaith and inter-community relations, two sites are of particular interest:

<www.christianmuslimforum.org> is an excellent resource which, *inter alia*, showcases innovative local, regional and national examples of active collaboration between Christians and Muslims, especially young people.

<www.aauk.org/> is the webste of Alif Aleph, which exists to promote contacts between British Muslims and British Jews.

Index